Street Smart Money

The Hustler's Guide to Financial Freedom

by

Connor Victorious

Felony Freedom Publishing

An Independent Publishing House

ISBN:9798856884875

Cover design by: kingweeble

Printed in the United States of America

To the fallen...

"Let your success make the noise, but hustle in silence."

- Old Mafia Saying

Contents

Preface

As I sit here, penning these words, I can't help but reflect on the incredible journey that led me to write "Hustle & Prosper: A Street-Smart Guide to Personal Finance." Allow me to introduce myself - I am Connor Victorious, an author with a colorful past that I wear as a badge of honor. But this book isn't just about me; it's about all of us, the hustlers who've faced adversities and emerged stronger, wiser, and ready to stack wealth.

The inspiration for this guide comes from my own transformational journey. You see, not too long ago, I was knee-deep in the world of street hustles and crime. But life has a funny way of presenting us with unexpected opportunities, and I found myself at a crossroads. It was either continue down a path of destruction or turn my life around and embrace a new purpose.

The choice was clear – I decided to rewrite my destiny.

Thus, "Street Smart Money" was born. I wanted to share my experiences and the lessons I've learned on this tumultuous but empowering ride. It's not just about telling my story; it's about empowering you to reclaim control of your financial life, just like I did. I've walked the gritty streets, and I've faced obstacles that seemed insurmountable. But I also discovered that the same tenacity that fueled my street hustles could be channeled into building a brighter financial future.

The writing process was a cathartic journey for me, delving into the depths of my past while crafting a roadmap to financial success. It was essential for me to keep the language authentic and relatable, using urban slang and modern grammar to create a connection with readers from all walks of life. I wanted this book to resonate with anyone who's ever felt trapped in their circumstances but still had that fire to rise above.

As I wrote, I couldn't ignore the historical context surrounding the material. The struggle for financial prosperity is not new; it has plagued communities for generations. But by drawing parallels between the streets and personal finance, we can understand that the principles of hustlin' are universal. The quest for generational wealth and the desire to leave a positive mark on the world have driven individuals from different backgrounds for centuries.

The purpose of this book is clear - to empower you, the reader, to take control of your financial destiny and thrive. I want you to find inspiration in my journey, not as a glorification of a criminal past, but as a testament to the power of transformation and growth. This is a guide for those ready to embrace financial literacy, hustlin' legally, and leaving a legacy that extends beyond their own lifetime.

And now, let me introduce you to the heart and soul of this guide—Max "Stacks" Johnson. You might be wonderin', why is this book narrated by a character named Max "Stacks" Johnson? Well, let me tell ya, it's not just 'cause it sounds cool (even though it does!). Max "Stacks" Johnson is the brainchild of my creative alter ego, a street-smart hustler with a knack for stackin' that paper.

When I set out to write this guide, I knew I needed a voice that could connect with all the hustlers out there. And who better to do that than Max "Stacks" Johnson? He's the perfect embodiment of the hustle mentality, with a street-wise flair that'll keep you hooked from the first page.

Max has seen it all, from the gritty streets to financial success, and he's not shy about sharing the ups and downs of his journey. Through his witty remarks and unique perspective, he'll keep you entertained while droppin' knowledge bombs like nobody's business.

But don't let his tough exterior fool ya - Max "Stacks" Johnson has a heart of gold. He's not just here to teach you how to hustle and prosper; he's here to inspire and uplift you on your own path to financial greatness.

So, strap in and get ready to roll with Max "Stacks" Johnson as your guide. Together, we'll hustle, stack, and prosper like never before. Let's dive into this street-smart guide to personal finance and unlock the secrets to financial success. And remember, with Max "Stacks" Johnson leadin' the way, you're in for one wild and enlightenin' ride!

- Connor Victorious

SECURE THE BAG

Born Hustlin'

Yo, what's good, fam? Buckle up because I'm about to take you on a journey down memory lane – back to the days when the sun seemed to shine a little less brightly, and life was as raw and real as it could get. It was in these rough and tumble streets that I came into this world, Max "Stacks" Johnson, a name that would soon be synonymous with the hustle game.

You see, the neighborhood I grew up in wasn't exactly a walk in the park. It was a place where dreams were deferred, and hope seemed like a distant memory. Money? Ha, it was like chasing shadows in an eternal dance. But in the midst of these hardships, I witnessed the grit and determination of my parents.

They worked tirelessly, breaking their backs to put food on the table and make ends meet. The lessons they taught me, the value of hard work, the importance of never giving up, became the cornerstones of my hustler's mentality.

At an age when other kids were playing with toys, I was already thinking about my next move. I wanted more than what this concrete jungle had to offer. I wanted to break free from the cycle of poverty and build something greater. So, armed with nothing but determination, I took my first steps into the world of hustling.

I started small, flipping candy and snacks at school, turning a few dollars into more. It wasn't much, but it was the spark that ignited a fire within me. I realized that in this world, you can either be a victim of circumstances or a master of your destiny. And I chose the latter.

The streets became my classroom, and every interaction was a lesson. I quickly learned that the world owed me nothing; I had to earn it, create my opportunities, and carve out my path. It was a dance between risk and reward, where failure was not a setback but a chance to refine my hustle.

A hustler's mentality is more than just a means to make money; it's an art form. It's about seeing potential where others see obstacles, spotting opportunities amidst chaos, and turning setbacks into stepping stones. It's about bending the world to your will, not accepting things as they are but shaping them into what they could be.

I hustled smart, understanding the value of timing. In the streets, you can't afford to wait for an invitation; you have to crash the party and make your presence known. I developed a keen eye for reading people, understanding their desires and needs, and positioning myself to deliver what they sought.

But let's keep it 100 – not every move I made back then was something to be proud of. Yeah, I got into some things that I'm not particularly eager to boast about, but those experiences molded me just as much as my successes did. They taught me the consequences of poor decisions, the weight of accountability, and the importance of making amends.

My journey wasn't a solitary one; I was surrounded by fellow hustlers and dreamers, each carving their own path to survival. We shared knowledge, skills, and support. It was a brotherhood, a community built on mutual respect and the understanding that we were in this together.

But this story isn't about glamorizing the streets; it's about recognizing that adversity breeds resilience. It's about acknowledging that the struggles we face in life can forge us into something greater. Being born hustlin' isn't about being born into a life of crime; it's about being born with a spirit that refuses to accept defeat, that refuses to settle for mediocrity.

As we delve deeper into this street-smart guide to personal finance, I want you to remember where we come from. We're not here to glorify the streets; we're here to celebrate the spirit that emerged from them. It's time to harness that hustler's mentality and apply it to the money game, to level up and secure our futures.

So, as we embark on this journey, remember this – we may have been born in the struggle, but we're destined for greatness. We're ready to hustle, grind, and stack those dollars, not just for the sake of having wealth, but for the power to shape our destinies, to uplift our communities, and to create a legacy that will transcend generations.

Let's hustle with purpose, let's hustle with integrity, and let's hustle with our eyes fixed on a brighter future. We got this, fam. So, grab your dreams, lace up your hustle boots, and let's set forth on a journey of financial success like no other. The streets might have raised us, but we're destined to rise above them and prosper. Get ready, 'cause we're just getting started!

In the beginning, it wasn't easy. The streets were unforgiving, and obstacles seemed to multiply like rabbits. But I didn't let that deter me. I saw every challenge as an opportunity to hone my skills, to sharpen my instincts. I learned how to adapt to ever-changing circumstances, like water flowing around rocks in a river. Hustling taught me to be versatile, to wear many hats, and to thrive in the face of uncertainty.

But it wasn't just about making money; it was about survival. It was about helping my family and my community rise above their circumstances. I understood that my success wasn't just my own; it was a beacon of hope for others. I knew that if I could make it, anyone could.

As I hustled my way through the maze of life, I began to realize that the power of the hustle lay not just in monetary gains but in the lessons it imparted. It taught me discipline, patience, and the importance of delayed gratification. It taught me that success wasn't an overnight affair; it was a result of consistent effort and unwavering dedication.

The streets can be harsh, and they can test your resolve, but they can also forge you into something greater. They can shape you into a person who refuses to settle for mediocrity, who sets audacious goals and is willing to do whatever it takes to achieve them. I knew that if I wanted to thrive, I had to embrace the hustle mentality fully.

In the pursuit of my dreams, I didn't always have a roadmap. But that's the beauty of the hustle – it teaches you to navigate the unknown, to chart your course through uncharted waters. I learned to trust my instincts, to follow my gut, and to listen to my inner voice. It wasn't always easy, but it was always worth it.

As I hustled my way through the ups and downs, I encountered people from all walks of life – some who supported me and others who tried to bring me down. But I didn't let the naysayers deter me. I knew that success attracts haters, and I wore their negativity as a badge of honor. After all, if you're not attracting haters, you're probably not doing something right.

Hustling also taught me the value of humility. It humbled me to realize that there was always more to learn, more to achieve. It taught me that no matter how successful I became, I should never forget where I came from and the struggles that shaped me. It was a reminder to remain grounded and to use my success to uplift others.

In the midst of the hustle, I also learned the art of balance. Hustling can be all-consuming, and it's easy to lose sight of what truly matters. But I made it a point to maintain a balance between work, family, and personal well-being. I knew that success wasn't just about the money; it was about finding fulfillment in every aspect of life.

Through it all, the hustle remained a source of strength and inspiration. It fueled my ambition and reminded me that nothing was impossible. It taught me that in life, we don't get what we wish for; we get what we work for. The hustle was a constant reminder that success wasn't handed to me on a silver platter; I had to grab it with both hands and hold on tight.

So, as we embark on this street-smart guide to personal finance, let's remember that we are all born hustlers in our own right. Whether we come from the streets or the suburbs, the hustle mentality resides within each of us. It's not just about making money; it's about taking charge of our lives, shaping our destinies, and leaving a lasting legacy.

Together, let's embrace the hustle and prosper like never before. Let's use this guide to tap into our inner hustler and unleash our full potential. As we flip through these pages, let's make a pact to hustle with passion, to stack with purpose, and to create a future that is as bright as the stars in the night sky.

The journey won't be easy, but nothing worth having ever is. There will be obstacles, setbacks, and moments of doubt. But we won't let that stop us. We'll hustle harder, dream bigger, and rise above every challenge that comes our way.

So, get ready, my fellow hustlers, because this is just the beginning. We're about to embark on a life-changing adventure, armed with the hustler's spirit, and fueled by the desire to create a life of abundance and prosperity. Together, we'll hustle, stack, and prosper like never before. Let's make it happen!

Chasin' that Bag

Now that you know a bit about where I come from and the essence of the hustler's mentality, it's time to delve deep into the next chapter of our journey – the art of "chasin' that bag." Trust me; this ain't your ordinary treasure hunt; it's a relentless pursuit of financial success, freedom, and abundance.

In the hustle game, chasin' that bag is the heartbeat of everything we do. It's not just about making money; it's about securing a future that allows us to live life on our terms, to break free from the shackles of financial stress, and to create opportunities for ourselves and our loved ones. It's about having the freedom to indulge in our passions, to experience the world, and to leave a legacy that lasts beyond our time.

But let's keep it real; chasin' that bag ain't a walk in the park. It's not a one-time sprint; it's a marathon. It requires relentless focus, unwavering determination, and a commitment to our financial goals. It's about being strategic and staying laser-focused on the bigger picture.

The first step in chasin' that bag is setting financial goals. You gotta know what you're aiming for; otherwise, you'll be running in circles without a destination. Your goals are your compass, guiding you through the twists and turns of the hustle game. They give you direction and purpose, and they fuel your drive to keep going, even when the going gets tough.

But setting goals isn't enough; you gotta stay focused. In the hustle game, distractions lurk around every corner, tempting you to veer off course. But you can't afford to lose sight of what truly matters. Keep your eye on the prize, fam, and don't let anything or anyone sway you from your path.

In the pursuit of our goals, we're gonna encounter challenges and obstacles. But remember, hustlers don't back down from a fight; we rise to the occasion. Embrace those challenges as opportunities for growth and self-discovery. It's in facing adversity that we become stronger, more resilient, and better equipped to navigate the ups and downs of the financial journey.

Now, I gotta drop some truth on you – chasin' that bag ain't just about waiting for opportunities to fall into your lap. Nah, it's about actively seeking those opportunities, about being proactive in creating your own luck. In the streets, we know that fortune favors the bold, and the same holds true in the financial game.

Look around you; there are opportunities everywhere – in the market, in the community, in your own skills and talents. It's all about recognizing them and having the courage to seize them. Don't wait for a golden ticket to land at your doorstep; go out there and make things happen.

You might be wondering, "Stacks, how do I identify these opportunities?" Well, my friend, it starts with being aware and staying informed. Knowledge is power in the hustle game. Stay up-to-date with current events, trends, and developments in the financial world. Learn from the successes and failures of others, and use that knowledge to inform your own decisions.

But hold up, chasin' that bag isn't just about making money; it's also about using it wisely. Being a smart hustler means being a smart steward of your finances. Budgeting is a word we don't throw around lightly in the streets, but trust me, it's essential. You gotta know where your money is going and how it's working for you.

Budgeting isn't about restricting yourself; it's about being intentional with your spending. It's about separating needs from wants and making conscious choices that align with your financial goals. Remember, every dollar you spend is an investment in your future, so make sure you're investing wisely.

Speaking of investments, as hustlers, we're all about making our money work for us. It's not just about what you earn; it's about what you keep and grow. That's where investing comes into play. I ain't talking about rolling dice in a back alley; I'm talking about legitimate, well-thought-out investments that have the potential to multiply your wealth over time.

Now, investing ain't a get-rich-quick scheme. It's a long game, and it requires patience and discipline. But trust me when I say that compound growth is a beautiful thing. It's like planting seeds in a garden – if you nurture them and let them grow, they'll bear fruit far beyond your expectations.

There are countless avenues for investing, from stocks and bonds to real estate and businesses. Each comes with its own set of risks and rewards, and it's essential to do your homework and seek advice from knowledgeable mentors. Remember, in the streets, we trust those who've been there before us, and the same principle applies to investing.

But let me tell you something crucial – don't just invest in money; invest in yourself. The hustle mentality is about constant growth and self-improvement. Take the time and resources to develop your skills, expand your knowledge, and enhance your value in the marketplace.

When you invest in yourself, you're laying the foundation for future success. You're equipping yourself with the tools and capabilities to seize even more significant opportunities down the road. So, never stop learning, never stop growing, and never underestimate the power of self-investment.

As we chase that bag, let's not forget that the journey is just as important as the destination. Embrace the hustle, relish the challenges, and celebrate the victories, no matter how small. This journey isn't just about making it to the finish line; it's about enjoying every step of the way.

Now, let's talk about patience – it's a virtue, my friend. Chasin' that bag might take time, and it might test your patience, but you can't let impatience derail your progress. Rome wasn't built in a day, and neither will your financial empire.

The hustle game is full of twists and turns, and sometimes, you might feel like you're taking one step forward and two steps back. But that's part of the process. Stay the course, and don't let temporary setbacks shake your resolve. Trust the process and trust in your ability to overcome any obstacle in your path.

I want you to remember this, fam – you're not alone on this journey. We're in this together, hustling side by side, learning from each other, and cheering each other on. Surround yourself with like-minded individuals who uplift and inspire you, who push you to be your best self.

And while we're on the topic of support, don't be afraid to ask for help when you need it. The hustle game can be tough, and sometimes, we all need a helping hand. Whether it's seeking financial advice, mentorship, or guidance, don't let pride stand in the way of your growth.

Chasin' that bag is about more than just financial gain; it's also about personal growth and fulfillment. As we navigate the ups and downs of the hustle, take the time to reflect on your journey. Celebrate the progress you've made, acknowledge the lessons you've learned, and appreciate the person you're becoming in the process.

And let's not forget to celebrate the wins, no matter how small. Each victory, no matter how insignificant it may seem, is a testament to your hard work and dedication. So, take a moment to pat yourself on the back and relish the joy of your achievements.

Now, as we continue chasin' that bag, keep in mind that balance is key. Hustling doesn't mean sacrificing everything else in your life. It's about finding harmony between your financial goals and your personal well-being. Take care of yourself, spend time with loved ones, and indulge in the things that bring you joy.

But at the same time, stay hungry and stay humble. The hustle game is ever-evolving, and there's always room for improvement. Continually reassess your goals, fine-tune your strategies, and adapt to changing circumstances. A hustler is never complacent; a hustler is always hungry for more.

So, my fellow hustlers, let's lace up our boots, tighten our shoelaces, and hit the ground running. We got dreams to chase, goals to crush, and bags to secure. It won't be easy, but nothing worth having ever is. But I can promise you this – with the hustler's mentality, anything is possible.

Let's go out there and chase that bag like we were born to do it. And remember, fam, the hustle isn't just about the destination; it's about enjoying the journey and becoming the best version of ourselves along the way. Together, we'll navigate the twists and turns, celebrate the victories, and overcome the challenges that come our way.

So, let's get out there and hustle like never before. We're on this journey together, and with the hustler's spirit in our hearts, we're unstoppable. Let's chase that bag, stack those dollars, and prosper like never before. The world is our playground, and the hustle is our game. Let's make it happen!

Show Me the Money

Alright, my hustlers, we've got our goals set, and we're locked in on chasin' that bag. Now, it's time to get down to the nitty-gritty – managing that money like a boss. We're gonna talk about budgeting, living within our means, and making sure we never find ourselves "broke as a joke."

In the streets, we know that money talks, and it's time to make sure it's speaking our language. Budgeting is a word that might not sound cool, but trust me, it's the backbone of financial success. Think of it as a roadmap, guiding you to your financial destination.

When I say budgeting, I ain't talking about depriving yourself of the things you love. It's not about living like a monk, surviving on bread and water. Nah, it's about being intentional with your spending and making sure every dollar has a purpose.

The first step in creating a budget is to track your expenses. Yeah, I know, it sounds tedious, but it's crucial. You gotta know where your money is going, so you can see where you can make adjustments and cut unnecessary spending.

Start by listing all your monthly expenses – rent, utilities, groceries, transportation, entertainment, the whole nine yards. Be honest with yourself, and don't forget those small expenses that add up quickly. Once you've got everything down on paper, it's time to do some calculations.

Take a good look at your income and subtract your expenses. What's left is what you have to work with. Now, it's decision time – allocate your money wisely. Prioritize your needs over your wants, and make sure your essential expenses are covered before splurging on the extras.

You see, in the streets, we know that the difference between success and failure often lies in the small choices we make. Skipping that daily latte might not seem like a big deal, but over time, those small savings add up to something significant. It's about making those smart, everyday choices that set us up for long-term success.

And don't forget about the unexpected expenses – life has a way of throwing curveballs at us. That's why it's essential to create an emergency fund. It's like having a safety net that catches you when you fall. Aim to save three to six months' worth of living expenses, so you're prepared for whatever comes your way.

Now, let's talk about living within your means. In the streets, we know that flashing cash might earn you some respect, but it's not a sustainable way to build wealth. It's about stacking those dollars, not blowing them on things that won't bring lasting value to your life.

Living within your means means being content with what you have while still working towards your goals. It's about being satisfied with a modest lifestyle, knowing that you're on the path to something greater. It's about being disciplined with your spending and not letting peer pressure or societal expectations dictate your financial choices.

In the hustle game, we know that patience is a virtue, and that holds true in managing your money. Building wealth takes time, and it requires discipline and consistency. It might be tempting to splurge on the latest gadgets or fashion trends, but ask yourself – is this really going to move me closer to my goals?

One thing I've learned from the streets is that material possessions might bring temporary satisfaction, but true fulfillment comes from achieving your dreams and building a secure future. So, focus on the long game, and don't let the allure of instant gratification distract you from your mission.

Now, let's talk about debt – it's like a heavyweight that can drag you down if you're not careful. In the streets, we know that owing someone else can make you feel like you're not in control. That's why we gotta be smart about managing debt. There's good debt and bad debt, and knowing the difference is essential. Good debt is an investment in your future – like taking out a loan for education or starting a business. Bad debt, on the other hand, is when you're borrowing to finance unnecessary expenses or things that depreciate in value.

If you've got bad debt, make it a priority to pay it off as soon as possible. Use any extra cash you have to tackle those high-interest debts first. It's like shedding weight off your shoulders and giving yourself the freedom to move forward.

But let's not forget about good debt – when managed responsibly, it can be a powerful tool. Take mortgages, for example. Buying a home can be a wise investment, as it builds equity and provides stability. Just make sure you're not overextending yourself and that you can comfortably handle the monthly payments.

Now, let's talk about credit scores – it's like a report card for your financial behavior. In the streets, we know that reputation matters, and a good credit score is essential for opening doors and securing better opportunities.

Your credit score is determined by factors like your payment history, credit utilization, length of credit history, and types of credit you have. Maintaining a good credit score shows lenders and potential partners that you're reliable and trustworthy.

Building good credit takes time, but it starts with being responsible with your credit cards and loans. Pay your bills on time, keep your credit utilization low, and avoid applying for multiple lines of credit within a short period. Remember, in the streets and in the financial game, a good reputation is priceless.

So, my fellow hustlers, as we navigate the world of personal finance, let's remember the principles that guide us – budget wisely, live within your means, build an emergency fund, manage debt responsibly, and maintain a good credit score. These are the building blocks of financial success, and they'll serve as the solid foundation for our future endeavors.

The hustle isn't just about making money; it's about managing it wisely and using it as a tool to create the life we envision. Let's stack those dollars like pros and show the world what we're made of. We're hustlers, and we're gonna make every dollar count. Get ready, fam, 'cause we're just getting started!

Credit Game Strong

Alright, my hustlers, it's time to level up our financial game and dive into the world of credit. In the streets, we know that a reputation can make or break you, and when it comes to personal finance, your credit score is your calling card. So, let's talk about building a credit game so strong that lenders and partners will be knocking on our doors.

In the hustle game, we know that trust and credibility matter. The same holds true in the financial world. Your credit score is like a report card that reflects your financial behavior. It tells lenders, landlords, and potential business partners how responsible you are with managing debt and repaying your obligations.

So, the first step in building a strong credit game is understanding what goes into your credit score. It's not some mysterious formula; it's a combination of factors that you have control over. The most significant components of your credit score are your payment history, credit utilization, length of credit history, types of credit, and recent credit applications.

Let's start with payment history – it's like the foundation of your credit game. Paying your bills on time is non-negotiable. Late payments can have a significant negative impact on your credit score, so make sure you always meet those due dates. Set reminders, automate payments if possible, do whatever it takes to stay on top of your bills.

Next up is credit utilization – it's like the percentage of your credit limit that you're using. In the streets, we know that living below our means is key to financial success. The same principle applies here – aim to keep your credit utilization below 30% of your total credit limit. High credit card balances can hurt your credit score, so focus on paying down those debts.

Now, let's talk about the length of your credit history – it's like the street cred you've built over time. The longer you've had credit accounts in good standing, the better it is for your credit score. That's why it's essential to maintain older accounts, even if you don't use them regularly. Closing old accounts can shorten your credit history and impact your score.

Diversifying your types of credit is like having multiple skills in the hustle game – it makes you more versatile and well-rounded. Having a mix of credit cards, loans, and lines of credit can positively impact your credit score. But remember, don't go on a credit spree just for the sake of variety. Only take on credit that you can manage responsibly.

And lastly, we gotta be mindful of recent credit applications – it's like the impression you leave when you're out there hustling for new opportunities. Applying for too much credit within a short period can signal financial instability to lenders. So, be strategic about when and where you apply for credit.

Building a strong credit game takes time and patience, but the results are worth it. A good credit score opens doors to better interest rates, lower insurance premiums, and increased chances of securing loans or business partnerships. It's like having the VIP pass in the financial world.

But hold up, let's not forget about credit reports – it's like the portfolio of your financial journey. You're entitled to a free credit report from each of the three major credit bureaus – Equifax, Experian, and TransUnion – every year. Review your credit reports regularly to check for errors or inaccuracies that could be dragging down your score.

If you find any mistakes, dispute them with the credit bureaus and get them corrected. A clean and accurate credit report is essential for maintaining a strong credit game.

Now, in the streets, we know that loyalty and trust go both ways. The same applies to the financial game. As you build a strong credit game, you'll find that lenders and credit card companies will be eager to reward you for your responsible behavior.

You might start receiving offers for better credit cards with lower interest rates, higher credit limits, or rewards programs. But remember, not every offer is a golden opportunity. Evaluate each offer carefully, consider the terms and conditions, and choose the ones that align with your financial goals.

But what if you're just starting and don't have much credit history? Well, in the streets, we know that sometimes you gotta prove yourself to earn trust. The same goes for building credit. If you're starting from scratch, consider options like secured credit cards or becoming an authorized user on someone else's credit card to begin building your credit history.

And let's talk about being responsible with credit cards – it's like having a balance between risk and reward in the hustle game. Credit cards can be powerful tools for building credit and earning rewards, but they can also lead to debt if not managed wisely.

Use credit cards responsibly, only charge what you can afford to pay off each month, and avoid carrying balances that accrue interest. Credit card debt can quickly spiral out of control, so be disciplined and only use credit cards as a means to build your credit game.

Now, in the streets, we know that there are sharks out there, waiting to take advantage of unsuspecting prey. The same holds true in the financial world. Beware of credit repair scams that promise to magically fix your credit overnight. There's no quick fix to building a strong credit game; it takes time, discipline, and responsible financial behavior.

So, my fellow hustlers, let's make it a mission to build a credit game so strong that it speaks volumes about our financial responsibility and trustworthiness. Keep those payments on time, watch that credit utilization, maintain a diverse credit portfolio, and review your credit reports regularly.

Future of abundance and prosperity.

Remember, a strong credit game is like a powerful asset in your financial arsenal. It opens doors to opportunities and sets you on the path to financial success. Let's hustle smart, build our credit game strong, and show the world that we're not just here to stack dollars – we're here to secure

Investin' in Yo' Future

Alright my hustlers, we've been mastering the art of budgeting, living within our means, and building a credit game so strong it's like our financial armor. Now, it's time to take things to the next level and talk about a game-changer in the hustle game – investing in yo' future.

In the streets, we know that money makes money, and investing is like planting seeds that grow into a bountiful harvest. It's the key to building wealth and securing a future of financial freedom. So, grab a seat, and let's dive into the world of investments.

Now, I know what some of you might be thinking – "Investing sounds complicated, Stacks. I ain't no Wall Street guru." But here's the thing, fam – you don't need a fancy suit or a degree in finance to be a successful investor. All you need is a little knowledge, some common sense, and the hustler's spirit.

At its core, investing is about putting your money to work for you. It's like hiring a team of workers who labor day and night to grow your wealth. And just like in the streets, you gotta be smart about who you hire.

So, let's talk about some investment options that can help us hustle our way to financial success:

Stocks

Investing in stocks is like owning a piece of a company. When you buy shares, you become a shareholder, and you have a stake in the company's success. As the company grows and makes profits, the value of your shares increases. Stocks can be a great way to build wealth over the long term.

Bonds

Bonds are like lending money to governments or corporations. In return, they pay you interest on the loan. Bonds are considered lower risk than stocks, and they provide a steady stream of income for investors.

Real Estate

In the streets, we know that property can be a valuable asset. Investing in real estate means buying properties to rent out or sell for a profit. Real estate can provide a source of passive income and can appreciate in value over time.

Mutual Funds

Mutual funds are like a team of investments bundled together. When you invest in a mutual fund, your money is pooled with other investors, and a professional fund manager handles the investments. Mutual funds offer diversification and are a good option for those who want a hands-off approach to investing.

Exchange-Traded Funds (ETFs)

ETFs are similar to mutual funds but trade on stock exchanges like individual stocks. They offer diversification and are an affordable way to invest in a wide range of assets.

Now, let me drop some truth on you – investing ain't a get-rich-quick scheme. It's a marathon, not a sprint. In the streets, we know that overnight success is rare, and the same principle applies to investing.

The key to successful investing is a long-term mindset. It's like planting a tree – it takes time for it to grow, but once it does, it provides shade and shelter for years to come. So, don't get discouraged if you don't see massive returns right away. Stay patient, stay consistent, and trust in the power of compound growth.

Speaking of compound growth, let me break it down for you – it's like earning interest on your interest. In the streets, we know that money attracts money, and compound growth is one of the most powerful forces in the financial game.

Let's say you invest $1,000 in a stock that earns a 10% return in the first year. By the end of the year, you'll have $1,100. But here's where the magic happens – in the second year, you'll earn a 10% return on $1,100, not just on the original $1,000. That means you'll have $1,210 by the end of the second year.

As time goes on, the power of compounding becomes even more evident. The longer you stay invested and reinvest your earnings, the faster your money grows. It's like a snowball effect – the more it rolls, the bigger it gets.

Now, in the streets, we know that putting all our eggs in one basket is a risky move. The same holds true in investing. Diversification is like having a diversified portfolio of skills – it reduces risk and increases the potential for reward.

Instead of putting all your money into one investment, spread it out across different assets and sectors. That way, if one investment takes a hit, it won't bring down your entire financial house of cards. Diversification is like an insurance policy against market volatility.

But hold up – let's not forget that investing comes with risks. Just like in the streets, there are no guarantees in the financial game. The value of investments can go up and down, and past performance doesn't guarantee future results.

That's why it's essential to do your homework and stay informed. Don't invest in something just because your cousin's friend's neighbor made a fortune on it. Do your research, understand the risks, and make informed decisions based on your financial goals and risk tolerance.

And remember, investing is not about getting rich quick. It's about building wealth over time. Set realistic expectations, and don't let short-term fluctuations in the market deter you from your long-term goals.

Now, in the streets, we know that timing is everything. The same holds true in the financial game. Trying to time the market – buying low and selling high – might sound like a smart move, but it's like trying to predict the weather. It's unpredictable and often leads to costly mistakes.

Instead of trying to time the market, focus on time in the market. Invest consistently and stay invested for the long haul. Trying to time the market is like trying to catch lightning in a bottle. It might happen once in a while, but it's not a reliable strategy for building wealth.

So, my fellow hustlers, let's take our financial game to the next level and start investing in yo' future. Remember, you don't need to be a Wall Street guru to succeed. Stay informed, diversify your investments, be patient, and trust in the power of compound growth.

And most importantly, remember that investing is like a journey – it's about learning, growing, and adapting along the way. Stay true to your financial goals, and never stop hustling for a future of abundance and prosperity. We got this, fam – let's stack those dollars and watch our investments grow like the champions we are!

Hustler's Side Hustles

Alright, my hustlers, we've been stacking those dollars, building our credit game strong, and investing in yo' future. But you know what they say – a true hustler never puts all their eggs in one basket. It's time to talk about side hustles – the secret weapon in a hustler's arsenal for maximizing income streams and reaching financial greatness.

In the streets, we know that the more skills you have, the more valuable you are. The same principle applies to the financial game. Side hustles are like additional talents that complement your main hustle and boost your earning potential.

Now, let me make one thing clear – side hustles ain't about hustling illegally or unethically. We're not talking about scamming or engaging in shady dealings. A hustler's side hustle is about leveraging your skills, passions, and resources to create legitimate and ethical income streams.

So, how do you find the perfect side hustle? Well, it starts with self-awareness. What are you good at? What do you enjoy doing in your spare time? What problems can you solve for others? These questions will help you identify potential side hustles that align with your strengths and interests.

In the streets, we know that time is money, and that's especially true when it comes to side hustles. Balancing a side hustle with your main hustle and personal life requires effective time management and discipline.

Don't bite off more than you can chew. Start small, and gradually scale up as you gain experience and confidence. Treat your side hustle like a business – set goals, create a schedule, and track your progress. Hustle smart, and you'll see your side hustle grow into a valuable income stream.

Now, let me drop some knowledge on you – not all side hustles are created equal. Some side hustles can earn you a few extra bucks, while others have the potential to become lucrative ventures that rival your main hustle.

In the streets, we know that diversifying your skills is like diversifying your portfolio – it reduces risk and increases opportunities. The same applies to side hustles. Don't put all your energy into one side hustle; explore different avenues and see what works best for you. Here are some hustler-approved side hustle ideas to get you started:

Freelancing

If you've got skills in writing, graphic design, web development, or any other creative field, freelancing can be a lucrative side hustle. You can find clients on platforms like Upwork, Fiverr, or even through networking.

Rideshare Driving

If you've got a car and a clean driving record, rideshare driving can be a flexible way to earn extra cash. It allows you to choose your own hours and work as much or as little as you want.

Online Selling

In the streets, we know that one man's trash is another man's treasure. Clean out your closet, garage, or attic, and sell items you no longer need on platforms like eBay or Facebook Marketplace.

Dog Walking or Pet Sitting

If you're an animal lover, pet-related side hustles can be a fun and rewarding way to make money. You can offer dog walking, pet sitting, or even grooming services in your neighborhood.

Renting out Your Space

If you've got an extra room or property, consider renting it out on platforms like Airbnb. It's like turning unused space into a profitable asset.

Teaching or Tutoring

If you're knowledgeable in a particular subject or skill, consider offering tutoring or teaching services. You can teach online or in-person, depending on your preference.

Social Media Management

In the digital age, businesses are always looking for help with social media. If you're savvy with Facebook, Instagram, or Twitter, you can offer social media management services to small businesses or influencers.

Event Planning

If you've got a knack for organizing and planning, event planning can be a rewarding side hustle. You can help people plan weddings, parties, or corporate events and earn a commission for your services.

Remember, in the streets and in the financial game, reputation is everything. Treat your side hustle like a business, deliver value to your customers, and build a strong brand that people trust and recommend.

But hold up – let's not forget the golden rule of side hustles: legality and ethics above all. Hustlers don't cut corners or engage in shady dealings. Your side hustle should complement your main hustle and contribute positively to your financial journey.

One thing I've learned from the streets is that networking is like building a network of connections. The same principle applies to side hustles. Don't be afraid to put yourself out there and market your side hustle. Leverage your existing network, use social media to promote your services, and attend networking events to meet potential clients.

And let me tell you something important – don't let your side hustle interfere with your main hustle. Your main hustle is like the foundation of your financial success, and you can't afford to neglect it. Make sure you strike a balance between your main hustle, side hustle, and personal life.

Now, in the streets, we know that not every side hustle will be a home run. Some side hustles might not work out as expected, and that's okay. Treat every experience as a learning opportunity, and don't be afraid to pivot and try something new.

The beauty of side hustles is that they allow you to experiment and discover new passions and skills. So, don't be discouraged by setbacks; embrace them as part of your journey to success.

In the financial game, we know that every dollar counts, and side hustles are like the extra points that add up to a winning score. So, my fellow hustlers, let's hustle smart, diversify our skills, and embrace the power of side hustles to maximize our earning potential.

Remember, the streets and the financial game are ever-changing, and we gotta stay adaptable and open to new opportunities. Keep hustling, keep learning, and watch those income streams multiply like a boss. Let's make every dollar count, and hustle our way to a future of financial abundance and prosperity!

Stackin' 101

Saving & Emergency Funds

Alright, my hustlers, by now, we've mastered the art of budgeting, built a credit game strong enough to open doors, invested in yo' future like financial ninjas, diversified our income streams with side hustles, and built our financial arsenal with savings. Now, it's time to delve even deeper into the world of stacking those dollars and creating rock-solid emergency funds.

In the streets, we know that the unexpected can hit us when we least expect it. That's why we gotta be prepared for whatever life throws our way. Having a solid saving game is like having a shield that protects us from financial hardships. Whether it's a medical emergency, unexpected job loss, or a major car repair, having savings can give us the peace of mind to navigate life's challenges without falling into financial distress.

So, let's start with the basics – why is saving important? Saving is like putting money in a piggy bank, except this piggy bank grows with interest. It's about setting aside a portion of your income for future use and building a safety net for both short-term and long-term goals.

In the mean streets of America, we know that every dollar counts, and saving is all about making those dollars work for us. The first step is to pay yourself first. Treat saving like a non-negotiable expense, just like paying rent or utilities. Set a savings goal and make it a priority to contribute to your savings regularly.

One way to make saving painless is through automation. Set up automatic transfers from your checking account to your savings account on payday. That way, you won't even miss the money, and your savings will grow steadily over time.

Now, let me drop some wisdom on you – saving isn't about hoarding money under your mattress like a treasure chest. It's about putting your money to work in the most efficient way possible. That's where interest comes into play.

In the financial game, we know that interest is like magic – it makes our money grow without lifting a finger. Whether it's through a high-yield savings account or a certificate of deposit (CD), earning interest on your savings can significantly boost your financial game.

We know that every dollar has a purpose, and that's especially true when it comes to saving. Start by setting clear and achievable saving goals. It could be building an emergency fund, saving for a down payment on a home, or funding a dream vacation.

Having specific goals gives your saving game direction and motivation. Break down your goals into smaller milestones and celebrate each victory along the way. It's like reaching checkpoints in the hustle game – each one brings you closer to the finish line.

Now, let's talk about emergency funds – they're like insurance policies for life's unexpected events. In the streets, we know that being prepared is key to survival. The same principle applies to our financial game.

An emergency fund is like a stash of cash reserved for emergencies only – like medical emergencies, car repairs, or sudden job loss. It's a safety net that prevents you from relying on credit cards or loans when life throws you a curveball.

Rainy days are inevitable, and having an emergency fund is like carrying an umbrella wherever you go. Ideally, aim to save three to six months' worth of living expenses in your emergency fund. This ensures you're prepared for any storm that comes your way.

Building an emergency fund takes time and discipline, but trust me, it's worth it. Start by setting a monthly savings goal for your emergency fund and treat it like any other financial priority. Don't be discouraged if you can't reach the full amount right away; every dollar counts, and you'll get there with persistence.

What about where to stash your savings, you ask? In the streets, we know that not all hiding spots are created equal. The same applies to saving – where you put your money matters.

For short-term goals and emergency funds, a high-yield savings account is a solid choice. It offers higher interest rates than traditional savings accounts, and your money remains easily accessible.

For long-term goals, like retirement or buying a home, consider investing your savings in assets that have the potential to grow over time. The earlier you start investing, the more time your money has to compound and grow.

But hold up – let's not forget that saving is like a marathon, not a sprint. It requires discipline and consistency, and there might be times when you face financial challenges that make saving difficult. That's when the hustler's spirit comes into play.

Out here, in these streets, we know that when the going gets tough, the tough get going. The same holds true in the financial game. If you encounter setbacks, stay focused on your goals, and be willing to adjust your plans as needed. Hustlers are adaptable and resourceful, and we can overcome any obstacle that comes our way.

> **Remember, in the streets and in the financial game, every dollar counts, and saving is the secret weapon to securing a future of abundance and prosperity. So, my fellow hustlers, let's stack those dollars like pros, create a safety net with emergency funds, and hustle our way to a future of financial security and success.**

Now, let's dive even deeper into the world of saving and emergency funds. In the streets, we know that every dollar counts, and that's especially true when it comes to saving. Saving is like building a fortress around our finances, protecting us from life's unexpected curveballs.

In the financial game, we know that it's not just about how much you make; it's also about how much you keep. Having a solid saving game is like having a secret weapon in the hustle game – it sets us up for long-term success.

But let me drop some real talk on you – saving ain't always easy. In the streets, we face temptations and distractions at every corner, and the same applies to our finances. There will always be that shiny new gadget or the latest fashion trend calling our name.

That's where discipline comes into play. In the streets, we know that discipline is like the foundation of success. The same holds true in the financial game. It's about making conscious choices and being mindful of our spending habits.

One way to boost your saving game is to track your expenses. Keep a record of every dollar you spend for a month, and you'll be surprised at how those small daily expenses add up. It's like shining a light on your financial habits – once you see where your money is going, you can make better choices about how to allocate it.

In the streets, it's understood that staying focused on our goals is essential. The same principle applies to saving. Set specific saving goals and keep them front and center in your mind. Whether it's saving for a dream vacation, buying a car, or building an emergency fund, having clear goals will keep you motivated and on track.

Now, let's talk about budgeting – it's like the blueprint for our financial success. In the streets, we know that a plan is essential for any operation. The same applies to our finances. A budget is like a roadmap that tells your money where to go.

Create a budget that aligns with your financial goals and stick to it like a pro. Include savings as a non-negotiable expense, just like paying your bills. It's like paying yourself first and putting your financial future at the top of the priority list.

In the financial game, we know that saving isn't just about the short term – it's also about the long term. That's where retirement savings come into play. Retirement might seem like a distant dream, but it's like investing in your future self.

Start saving for retirement as early as possible. In the streets, we know that time is money, and the same principle applies to retirement savings. The earlier you start, the more time your money has to grow and work for you.

We know that retirement savings are like building a fortress for our golden years. Consider opening a retirement account, like a 401(k) or an Individual Retirement Account (IRA). These accounts offer tax advantages and can help you grow your retirement savings faster.

Now, let's talk about the rainy days. In the streets, we know that unexpected things can happen at any time. That's where emergency funds come in – they're like financial insurance for life's unexpected events.

An emergency fund is like a stash of cash reserved for emergencies only – like medical emergencies, car repairs, or sudden job loss. It's a safety net that prevents you from relying on credit cards or loans when life throws you for a loop.

In the financial game, we know that rainy days are inevitable, and having an emergency fund is like carrying an umbrella wherever you go. Ideally, aim to save three to six months' worth of living expenses in your emergency fund. This ensures you're prepared for any storm that comes your way.

Building an emergency fund takes time and discipline, but trust me, it's worth it. Start by setting a monthly savings goal for your emergency fund and treat it like any other financial priority. Don't be discouraged if you can't reach the full amount right away; every dollar counts, and you'll get there with persistence.

Now, let's talk about where to stash your savings. In the streets, we know that not all hiding spots are created equal. The same applies to saving – where you put your money matters.

For short-term goals and emergency funds, a high-yield savings account is a solid choice. It offers higher interest rates than traditional savings accounts, and your money remains easily accessible.

For long-term goals, like retirement or buying a home, consider investing your savings in assets that have the potential to grow over time. The earlier you start investing, the more time your money has to compound and grow.

But hold up – let's not forget that saving is like a marathon, not a sprint. It requires discipline and consistency, and there might be times when you face financial challenges that make saving difficult. That's when the hustler's spirit comes into play.

In the streets, we know that when the going gets tough, the tough get going. The same holds true in the financial game. If you encounter setbacks, stay focused on your goals, and be willing to adjust your plans as needed. Hustlers are adaptable and resourceful, and we can overcome any obstacle that comes our way.

Remember, in the streets and in the financial game, every dollar counts, and saving is the secret weapon to securing a future of abundance and prosperity. So, my fellow hustlers, let's stack those dollars like pros, create a safety net with emergency funds, and hustle our way to a future of financial security and success.

But we're not done yet – there's more to learn and explore in the world of financial savvy. So, buckle up, my hustlers, because the journey to financial greatness is just getting started. Let's keep hustling, keep saving, and keep building our financial fortress one dollar at a time. Together, we'll conquer the financial game and secure a future of financial freedom and prosperity!

Financial Security

Alright, my fellow hustlers, we've come a long way in this journey towards financial greatness. We've learned the art of budgeting, mastered the credit game, invested like pros, hustled with side gigs, stacked those dollars in savings, and built emergency funds to weather any storm. But there's one more essential aspect of the financial game we must conquer – protecting our hard-earned money and ensuring our financial security.

In the streets, we know that safety is paramount. It's not just about physical safety; financial security is equally crucial. Just as we'd protect ourselves from potential threats on the streets, we must safeguard our finances from scams and frauds in the financial game.

The first golden rule of financial security is simple but vital – never share your personal and financial information with strangers or unverified sources. Just as we wouldn't trust every passerby on the streets, we must be cautious of unsolicited phone calls, emails, or messages asking for personal information, such as your social security number, bank account details, or passwords. Scammers are like chameleons, always adapting their tactics to catch you off guard, so always verify the authenticity of any request before sharing sensitive information.

In the financial game, knowledge is power. The more informed you are about common scams and frauds, the better equipped you'll be to protect yourself. Stay updated on the latest scams and learn to recognize red flags, like promises of quick and easy money, high-pressure tactics, or requests for upfront payments.

Now, let's talk about the keys to your financial fortress – passwords. In the streets, we know that a strong lock is essential to keep our valuables safe. The same principle applies to passwords. Create unique and robust passwords for all your financial accounts, and avoid using common or easily guessable phrases.

Consider using a password manager to keep track of your passwords securely. And never, ever share your passwords with anyone – not even your closest allies. In the financial game, your passwords are like the secret codes that protect your financial empire.

In the streets, we know that trust is earned through actions, not words. The same applies to financial institutions. Choose reputable and trustworthy banks or financial service providers for your accounts and investments. Look for institutions with strong security measures and a history of excellent customer service.

When it comes to financial advisors or investment opportunities, do your due diligence and verify their credentials and track record. Avoid falling for "get-rich-quick" schemes or investments that promise unrealistically high returns. Remember, if it sounds too good to be true, it probably is. In the financial game, hustlers make smart and calculated moves, not impulsive decisions based on empty promises.

In the streets, we know that sometimes, unexpected things can slip through the cracks. That's why having yo' back covered with insurance is crucial. Insurance is like a safety net that protects you from unexpected financial blows.

Consider having health insurance to cover medical expenses, car insurance to protect your vehicle, and homeowner's or renter's insurance to safeguard your belongings. It's like having a shield that guards you from financial disasters.

But insurance isn't just about protecting your physical assets; it's also about securing your financial future. Consider life insurance to provide for your loved ones in the event of your passing. Life insurance is like leaving a legacy that takes care of those you leave behind.

In the financial game, we know that vigilance is key to staying ahead of potential threats. Regularly review your financial statements, bank transactions, and credit reports. Check for any suspicious activity and report it immediately. In the streets, we're always alert, and the same holds true for your finances.

Now, let's talk about the importance of resilience. In the streets, we know that sometimes, life can throw us a curveball. That's why hustlers are always prepared to bounce back from setbacks. In the financial game, we call it resilience – the ability to stay strong in the face of challenges.

Whether it's a financial setback, a job loss, or a market downturn, remember that setbacks are temporary. Stay focused on your long-term goals, adjust your plans as needed, and keep hustling forward. In the streets, we don't back down from challenges, and the same spirit applies to your financial game.

In the financial game, we know that sometimes, the best defense is a good offense. That's where estate planning comes into play. Estate planning is like strategizing for the future, ensuring that your assets are distributed according to your wishes.

Consider creating a will or a living trust to designate how you want your assets to be distributed after your passing. It's like leaving a roadmap for your loved ones to follow, so they know how to manage your estate.

Now, let's talk about the power of financial literacy. In the streets, we know that knowledge is the key to success. The same applies to the financial game. Educate yourself about personal finance, investing, and money management.

Attend workshops, read books, and follow reputable financial experts. In the financial game, hustlers are always hungry for knowledge, and it's the ultimate tool for making informed and strategic decisions.

In the streets, we know that unity is strength. The same holds true in the financial game. Surround yourself with a supportive network of family, friends, and mentors who have your back. Share your knowledge and experiences with others, and learn from their wisdom. In the financial game, hustlers uplift each other and work together to achieve greatness.

Now, let's talk about the power of giving back. In the streets, we know that helping others is a sign of strength, not weakness. The same principle applies to the financial game. Consider charitable giving as a way to make a positive impact on your community and the world.

Support causes that are meaningful to you, whether it's education, healthcare, or environmental conservation. In the financial game, hustlers don't just accumulate wealth; we use our resources to uplift others and create a legacy of positive change.

In the streets, we know that sometimes, the best way to protect ourselves is to be proactive. That's why having a rainy-day fund is crucial. In the financial game, we call it an emergency fund – a stash of cash reserved for unexpected expenses.

Life can throw us curveballs, like medical emergencies, car repairs, or sudden job loss. Having an emergency fund is like carrying an umbrella wherever you go. It ensures you're prepared for any storm that comes your way.

Building an emergency fund takes time and discipline, but trust me, it's worth it. Start by setting a monthly savings goal for your emergency fund and treat it like any other financial priority. Don't be discouraged if you can't reach the full amount right away; every dollar counts, and you'll get there with persistence.

In the streets, we know that sometimes, it takes a team effort to achieve greatness. The same holds true in the financial game. Consider working with a financial advisor or planner to help you navigate the complexities of investing, retirement planning, and estate management.

A financial advisor is like having a seasoned coach in your corner, guiding you towards your financial goals. They can help you create a personalized financial strategy, manage your investments, and stay on track towards financial success.

In the financial game, hustlers are always willing to learn and adapt. Stay updated on the latest financial trends and economic developments. Attend seminars, webinars, and conferences to expand your knowledge.

In the streets, we know that being prepared is the key to success. The same principle applies to the financial game. Create a financial plan that aligns with your goals and values. Review and update your plan regularly as your life circumstances and financial goals evolve.

In the financial game, hustlers take control of their destiny. We don't leave our financial future to chance – we actively shape it with smart and strategic choices.

So, my fellow hustlers, let's protect yo' neck in the financial game like the savvy hustlers we are. Be cautious, stay informed, and take control of yo' financial destiny. Together, we'll navigate the dangerous waters of the financial game with wisdom and resilience. We got this – let's hustle and secure our financial success like true champions!

Entrepreneurial Vibes

Startin' Yo' Biz

Yo, welcome to the chapter that's all about unleashing your inner hustler and tapping into your entrepreneurial vibes. You see, in the streets, being your own boss is like the holy grail of hustlin', and in the financial game, starting your own business is like takin' control of your destiny. So, grab your hustler hat, 'cause we're about to dive deep into the world of entrepreneurship like true visionaries.

Startin' a business ain't for the faint of heart. Nah, it takes guts, dedication, and a whole lot of hustle. We know that challenges and setbacks are part of the game, but us hustlers, we don't back down – we embrace 'em and turn 'em into opportunities. It's like in the streets, where every obstacle is just another chance to level up.

It all starts with an idea, man – a vision that sets your soul on fire. It's that burning desire to create somethin' fresh, to solve problems, or to make a real difference in this crazy world. You gotta define that vision and refine it till it's sharper than a switchblade. Take the time to dig deep and understand what you're truly passionate about and what impact you want to make.

But before you dive in, lemme drop some street knowledge on you. Startin' a business ain't no walk in the park. You gotta do your research – know your industry, scope out the competition, and understand them potential customers. You gotta figure out what makes you stand out in this crazy crowded world. In the streets, we know that knowing your competition is the key to staying ahead of the game.

Then, craft that business plan like it's your masterpiece. A plan that lays out your goals, your strategies, and how you gonna stack them dollars. It's like your battle strategy, keepin' you on track to claim that victory. But don't just rush through it. Take the time to analyze your strengths and weaknesses, and map out the steps you need to take to make your vision a reality.

Now, let's talk about the money game. Every move counts, man. Consider your startup costs and how you gonna get that paper flowin'. You gotta be resourceful, just like in the streets. Hustlers find creative ways to make dreams a reality. If you need funding, don't be afraid to explore different options like loans, investors, or even crowdfunding.

Once you got that plan, you gotta register your business, protect it from the leeches, and keep them finances separate from your personal stash. Every dollar matters, and you gotta be smart with them moves. Get all the necessary permits and licenses in place, and don't forget about taxes, man. In the streets, we know that you gotta handle your business if you wanna stay out of trouble.

Develop a strong brand identity that speaks to your vision and connects with your target audience. You gotta stand out like a boss, makin' 'em remember you. Your brand is like your reputation in the streets – it's what people will remember you by.

Build your dream team of passionate and talented individuals who believe in your vision. Surround yourself with people who complement your strengths and compensate for your weaknesses. In the streets, we know that unity is strength, and in business, it's no different. A strong team is like having an army of hustlers working towards a common goal.

Be a master negotiator and get the best deals for your business. Every dollar saved is like money earned, and hustlers know how to hustle for them dollars. When dealing with suppliers or partners, don't be afraid to negotiate for better terms or prices. In the streets, we know that every dollar counts, and the same principle applies in the business world.

Now, let's talk about marketing, my friend. Visibility is everything. You gotta show up, show out, and make sure your target audience knows you exist. Use social media, content marketing, and networkin' like a boss. But remember, it's not just about the quantity of your marketing efforts – it's about the quality and the impact you make.

You gotta connect with your audience on a deeper level. In the streets, we know that building trust is crucial in any relationship. The same goes for your customers. Offer value, engage with them, and listen to their needs. Your marketing efforts should reflect your brand's personality and the unique solutions you offer.

Embrace innovation and stay open to new ideas and technologies. The world is constantly changing, and you gotta adapt and improve to meet them ever-changin' needs of your customers. In the streets, we know that sometimes, you gotta pivot. The same holds true in business. If something ain't workin', don't be afraid to change course and try something new.

But, we ain't done yet. You gotta stay on top of your finances, man. Cash flow is like the blood flow of your business. In the streets, we know that keepin' track of them dollars is essential. Same goes for your business. You gotta monitor your income and expenses, make sure you're staying within your budget, and plan for any financial challenges that may arise.

You gotta be vigilant about your cash flow and make smart financial decisions. In the streets, we know that every move you make can have consequences, and the same is true in business. You gotta be disciplined with your spending and avoid wasteful expenses. At the same time, you should invest strategically to grow your business and increase your profits.

Networkin' is power, my friend. Connect with other players in the game, build relationships, and expand your opportunities. In the streets, we know that who you know can open doors for you, just like in the business world. Attend industry events, join online communities, and reach out to potential partners or mentors.

Keep yourself motivated and inspired. Surround yourself with those who lift you up and stay hungry for knowledge. In the streets, we know that knowledge is power, and in business, it's no different. Stay up to date with the latest trends, learn from successful entrepreneurs, and invest in your personal and professional growth.

Stay focused on your vision, man. Don't let distractions or short-term temptations knock you off course. In the financial game, hustlers know that the long game is what pays off. Keep that burning desire to succeed alive, and use it as fuel to keep going when things get tough.

Resilience is the name of the game, my friend. In the streets, we know that life can be rough, but we don't back down. In business, you gotta rise up and overcome, just like a true hustler. There will be challenges and setbacks along the way, but don't let them stop you from chasing your dreams.

Remember, building a successful business takes time and effort. It's a journey, not a sprint. Be patient, stay committed, and keep hustlin' every step of the way. Learn from your mistakes, adapt your strategies, and keep evolving. Just like in the streets, you gotta be agile and ready to switch up your game when necessary.

Don't be afraid to take risks, my friend. In the streets, we know that sometimes, you gotta take calculated risks to come out on top. The same is true in business. Be willing to step out of your comfort zone and try new things. This is how you grow and expand your horizons.

Surround yourself with a strong support network. In the streets, we know that you're only as strong as your crew. The same holds true in business. Build relationships with like-minded entrepreneurs, mentors, and advisors. They can offer guidance, support, and valuable insights to help you navigate the challenges of entrepreneursp.

Keep learning and growing. In the streets, we know that knowledge is power. The same is true in business. Continuously educate yourself about your industry, market trends, and new technologies. Attend workshops, seminars, and webinars. Read books and listen to podcasts from experts in your field. Stay hungry for knowledge, and yu'll be better equipped to make informed decisions for your business.

elebrate your successes, no matter how small they may seem. In the streets, we know that every win counts, no matter how minor it may appear. The same principle applies in business. Acknowledge your achievements and milestones. Treat yourself and your team for a job well done. Celebrate the progress you've made and use it as motivation to keep pushing forward.

And finally, remember why you started this journey in the first place. In the streets, we know that having a purpose is what keeps us going when times get tough. The same applies in business. Your passion and vision are what fuel your hustle. Let them guide you through the challenges and uncertainties. Stay true to yourself and your dreams, and you'll find the strength to keep hustlin' and building the business of your dreams.

So, my fellow hustlers, unleash your entrepreneurial vibes and take that first step towards building the business of your dreams. But remember, it ain't no easy road. It's gonna be tough, but with the heart of a hustler, you gonna conquer the business world like a true boss. Let's hustle and claim that success like the savvy entrepreneurs we are!

Money Moves

Negotiatin' and Savin'

on Deals

Alright, my fellow hustlers, welcome to Chapter 10 – where we dive deep into the art of makin' money moves like a seasoned player in the game. In the streets, we know that every dollar counts, and the same holds true in the world of personal finance. It's all about makin' smart choices, savin' those hard-earned dollars, and makin' every deal work in your favor.

Now, listen up, 'cause I'm about to drop some street-smart knowledge on you. Negotiation – it's like a dance where you gotta move smooth and quick, avoidin' them traps, and gettin' what you want. In the streets, we negotiate deals all the time – it's how we get the best prices, avoid trouble, and come out on top.

When it comes to money moves, negotiation skills are essential. Whether you're hagglin' over a purchase or negotiatin' a salary, it's all about gettin' the most value for your efforts. Remember, the worst they can say is no, and in the streets, we ain't afraid of rejection – we bounce back and try again.

In business, negotiatin' contracts and deals can be make-or-break for your success. You gotta be a smooth talker, but it's more than just talk – it's about knowin' your worth and what you bring to the table. In the streets, we know that confidence is key. Believe in yourself and what you're bringin' to the deal, and others will see your value too.

Research and preparation are your secret weapons. In the streets, we gather info before makin' moves – it's the same in business. Know the market, know your competition, and know what you want out of the deal. Arm yourself with knowledge, and you'll be ready to negotiate like a pro.

But remember, it's not just about gettin' the upper hand. In the streets, we know that buildin' relationships is important. The same applies in business. Negotiatin' is not about crushin' the other party – it's about findin' a win-win solution that benefits everyone involved.

Sometimes, you gotta be creative with your

> **negotiations. In the streets, we know that thinkin' outside the box can lead to big payoffs. It's the same in business – don't be afraid to propose unconventional solutions that could lead to mutual benefits.**

Now, let's talk about savin' those hard-earned dollars. In the streets, we know that it's not just about how much you make – it's about how much you keep. It's like stackin' your paper in a safe place where it can grow and work for you.

Budgetin' is like makin' a financial game plan. It's trackin' your income and expenses, understandin' where your money is goin', and makin' sure you're spendin' it on what truly matters. In the streets, we gotta know where every dollar goes – it's survival. In personal finance, it's about buildin' a solid foundation for your future.

And listen, be realistic with your budget. In the streets, we know that we can't pretend to be what we're not. In personal finance, it's the same – don't overspend or live beyond your means. Stay true to yourself and your financial situation.

Be smart with your credit, my friend. In the streets, we know that your rep is everything. In personal finance, your credit score is like your street rep. It's a reflection of your financial trustworthiness. Pay your bills on time, keep your credit utilization low, and avoid unnecessary debts.

Now, let's talk about savin' up for that rainy day – your emergency fund. In the streets, we know that life can be unpredictable, and havin' some cash stashed away can be a lifesaver. It's the same in personal finance – buildin' an emergency fund gives you peace of mind and protects you from unexpected setbacks.

And yo, don't forget about investin'. In the streets, we know that idle money don't grow. In personal finance, investin' is like plantin' seeds that grow into a money tree. Explore different investment options, like stocks, bonds, real estate, or even startin' your own business. The key is to diversify your portfolio and spread the risk.

Keepin' your money secure is crucial. In the streets, we know that protectin' what's ours is a top priority. In personal finance, safeguardin' your assets and personal information is just as important. Be wary of scams and fraud, and take steps to keep your financial info safe.

> **Money ain't just about stackin' paper for yourself. In the**

> **streets, we know that sharin' our success with the community is vital. In personal finance, it's no different. Use your money to uplift others, support causes you believe in, and give back to the community.**

Negotiatin' and savin' on deals — it's a skill that'll serve you well both in the streets and in your personal finance journey. In the streets, we know that every deal can make a difference, and it's the same in the financial game. Stay sharp, keep hustlin', and make them money moves like a true boss.

Now, let's dig deeper into the art of negotiation. In the streets, we learn to read people, their body language, and their intentions. It's like a sixth sense, helpin' us to gauge their next move. In business, be observant during negotiations. Listen carefully to what the other party is sayin' and watch for any hints of hesitation or interest.

Adaptability is key, my friend. In the streets, we know that every situation is different, and we gotta be flexible to thrive. The same principle applies to negotiation. Be ready to adjust your approach based on the person you're dealin' with and the circumstances at hand.

> **Don't rush the negotiation process. In the streets, we know that patience is a virtue. Take your time, build rapport, and don't be too eager to seal the deal. Sometimes, silence speaks louder than words. Let the other party process the information and make the first move.**

Now, let's talk about the power of saying no. In the streets, we know that we can't say yes to every offer that comes our way. The same applies in business. Know your limits and don't be afraid to walk away from a deal that doesn't align with your goals or values. It's better to wait for the right opportunity than to settle for somethin' that'll leave you regretful.

But, don't let rejection discourage you. In the streets, we know that not every deal goes our way, but we don't give up. In business, keep a positive mindset and stay focused on your goals. Learn from the experience and use it to improve your negotiation skills for the next time.

Buildin' relationships is crucial in the streets, and it's just as important in business. In the streets, we know that loyalty and trust are earned, not given. In negotiation, focus on creatin' a bond with the other party. Show them that you're reliable, honest, and committed to a successful partnership.

In the streets, we gotta be street-smart and street-wise. We don't fall for tricks or schemes that'll leave us empty-handed. In business, stay vigilant during negotiations. Watch out for any hidden fees or fine print that could turn a seemingly good deal into a bad one.

Now, let's switch gears and talk about savin' on deals. In the streets, we know that stretchin' your dollars is essential for survival. In personal finance, it's about buildin' wealth and financial security. So, how do we go about savin' those hard-earned dollars?

First, track your expenses. In the streets, we know that accountin' for every penny is essential for survivin'. In personal finance, recordin' your expenses gives you a clear picture of where your money is goin'. It helps you identify areas where you can cut back and save more.

But remember, savin' doesn't mean livin' like a miser. In the streets, we know that enjoyin' life is just as important as stackin' paper. In personal finance, findin' a balance between savin' and spendin' is key. Treat yourself occasionally, but keep it within your budget.

> **Be a savvy shopper, my friend. In the streets, we know how to find the best deals and bargains. In personal finance, look for discounts, coupons, and sales. Before makin' a purchase, compare prices from different vendors and choose the most cost-effective option.**

Now, let's talk about credit cards. In the streets, we know that flashin' cash can attract trouble. In personal finance, credit cards can be a double-edged sword. Use 'em responsibly, pay off your balances on time, and avoid carryin' too much debt. Credit cards can offer rewards and perks, but they can also lead to financial troubles if not managed wisely.

Stay mindful of impulse purchases. In the streets, we know that actin' on impulse can lead to trouble. In personal finance, think twice before makin' a spontaneous purchase. Ask yourself if it aligns with your needs and financial goals. Sometimes, sleepin' on a decision can save you from buyer's remorse.

Now, let's talk about one of the biggest savin' moves – negotiatin' your bills. In the streets, we know how to haggle for a better price. In personal finance, call up your service providers and negotiate for better rates. Whether it's your phone bill, cable package, or insurance premiums – ask if they can offer you a better deal. You'd be surprised how much money you can save with a simple phone call.

And listen, hustlers don't pay full price when they don't have to. In the streets, we know how to find the hook-up. In personal finance, always be on the lookout for discounts and special offers. Whether it's buyin' in bulk, usin' coupons, or takin' advantage of seasonal sales – find ways to save money whenever you can.

Now, let's switch gears and talk about investin' in yourself. In the streets, we know that self-improvement is vital for survivin'. In personal finance, investin' in your skills and knowledge can lead to financial growth and career advancement.

Take courses, attend workshops, and seek out mentorship opportunities. In the streets, we learn from those who came before us, and in personal finance, learn from those who've achieved financial success. Seek guidance from financial experts and successful entrepreneurs, and apply their wisdom to your own journey.

In the streets, we know that every opportunity counts. In personal finance, seize opportunities for career advancement and salary increases. Be proactive in negotiatin' for better pay and benefits. Advocate for yourself and don't be afraid to ask for what you deserve.

> **Stay open to new opportunities and be ready to adapt to changes in the financial landscape. In the streets, we know that the game can change at any moment, and we gotta be ready to pivot. In personal finance, stay informed about market trends and economic shifts. Be flexible with your investment strategies and adjust them as needed.**

Now, let's talk about savin' for your future. In the streets, we know that stackin' paper for the long haul is vital. In personal finance, it's about buildin' financial security and a comfortable retirement.

Set long-term financial goals, like buyin' a house, savin' for your children's education, or retirin' early. In the streets, we know that havin' goals keeps us focused and driven. The same applies in personal finance – set clear goals and create a plan to achieve them.

Consider retirement savings plans like 401(k)s or IRAs. In the streets, we know that we gotta prepare for the future. In personal finance, start savin' for retirement as early as possible. The power of compound interest can turn small contributions into a significant nest egg over time.

Automate your savings, my friend. In the streets, we know that you gotta stash your cash where it's safe. In personal finance, set up automatic transfers to your savings or retirement accounts. This way, you won't forget to save, and it becomes a habit.

> **But remember, savin' for your future doesn't mean sacrificin' your present. In the streets, we know that life is too short not to enjoy it. In personal finance, find a balance between savin' for your goals and enjoyin' the present moment.**

Now, let's talk about the power of givin' back. In the streets, we know that community matters. In personal finance, use your financial success to uplift others and support causes you believe in.

Whether it's donatin' to charity, volunteerin' your time, or investin' in social enterprises, find ways to make a positive impact in your community. In the streets, we know that we rise by liftin' others. The same principle applies in personal finance – use your success to empower others and create a ripple effect of positive change.

In the streets, we know that buildin' connections is vital for survival. In personal finance, networkin' can open doors to new opportunities and collaborations. Attend industry events, join professional organizations, and connect with like-minded individuals.

Build relationships with mentors and advisors who can offer guidance and support on your financial journey. In the streets, we know that we learn from those who've been in the game longer than us. The same holds true in personal finance – seek guidance from those with more experience and knowledge.

> **Invest in your financial education, my friend. In the streets, we know that knowledge is power. In personal finance, stay informed about financial trends, investment strategies, and market shifts. Attend workshops, read books, and listen to podcasts from financial experts.**

Now, let's talk about resilience. In the streets, we know that life can be rough, but we don't back down. In personal finance, face financial challenges with the same tenacity. Life is full of ups and downs, and it's essential to stay resilient during tough times.

In the streets, we know how to adapt and survive. In personal finance, be prepared for financial setbacks and have a plan in place to bounce back. Create an emergency fund to cover unexpected expenses and protect yourself from financial hardships.

Now, let's talk about the ultimate money move – buildin' generational wealth. In the streets, we know that leavin' a legacy is essential. In personal finance, focus on creatin' long-term wealth that'll benefit future generations.

Invest in assets that appreciate over time and can be passed down to your children and grandchildren. In the streets, we know that hustlin' is about more than just survivin' – it's about thrivin' and leavin' a mark on the world. The same applies in personal finance – build a legacy that'll empower your family and community for years to come.

So, my fellow hustlers, as we wrap up this chapter, remember that negotiatin' and savin' on deals is a skill that'll serve you well in both the streets and your personal finance journey. Stay sharp, keep hustlin', and make them money moves like a true boss.

And most importantly, never forget your roots. In the streets, we know that success is sweeter when we bring others along with us. In personal finance, use your financial success to uplift those around you. Together, we can create a world where everyone has the opportunity to hustle, stack, and prosper. Let's keep on hustlin' and claim that success like the savvy entrepreneurs we are!

Dolla Bills & Taxes

Alright, my fellow hustlers, welcome to Chapter 11 – where we tackle one of the most inevitable aspects of our financial journey: taxes. In the streets, we know that money comes and goes, but taxes are like an unwelcome visitor that never seems to leave. But fear not, my friends, 'cause I'm here to break it down for you in street-style, so you'll be ready to face the tax game like a true boss.

In the streets, we know that ignorance ain't an excuse. The same principle applies to taxes. You gotta understand the basics of how it all works. Now, let me break it down for you in a language we can all relate to.

First things first, you gotta know your tax bracket. In the streets, we know that different territories have different rules, and it's the same with taxes. The government divides us into different income brackets, each with its own tax rate. The more you earn, the higher the percentage of your income you'll pay in taxes.

Alright, listen up, my fellow hustlers. When it comes to taxes, you gotta know your tax bracket like the back of your hand. Just like in the streets, different territories got different rules, and it's no different with taxes.

The government, they got this fancy system where they divide us into different income brackets. Each bracket got its own tax rate, and let me tell you, it ain't no joke. The more money you bring in, the higher the percentage they gonna take from you.

So, if you out there hustlin' hard and stackin' paper like a boss, be ready to hand over a bigger chunk of your earnings to the taxman. They call it a progressive tax system, but to us, it just means they gonna take more when you earn more.

But hey, don't get me wrong, it ain't all bad. See, if you smart with your money, you can find ways to stay in a lower tax bracket. That means keepin' your taxable income in check, so they don't take too much from you.

Now, I ain't sayin' you should be afraid of makin' money, nah. We hustlers, we aim high, and we gonna get that bag. But you gotta be savvy about it. Know the tax game, know where you stand, and make strategic moves to keep as much of your hard-earned cash as possible.

Remember, the taxman, they always watchin'. They ain't gonna let you slide if you try to play 'em. So, be legit with your money, report all your earnings, and make sure you're in the right tax bracket.

In the streets, we know how to adapt and survive. The same goes for taxes. If you wanna stay on top of the game, you gotta know the rules and play 'em smart. So, do your homework, keep your finances in order, and don't let the taxman catch you slippin'. Stay sharp and keep hustlin'!

Now, let's talk about deductions. In the streets, we know how to keep what's rightfully ours. In taxes, deductions are like the shortcuts that lower your taxable income. They come in various forms, from medical expenses to charitable contributions. So, keep track of your expenses and see if you qualify for any deductions that can save you some dough.

Now, you might be wonderin' what these deductions are all about. Well, they come in all shapes and sizes, just like our hustles on the streets. From medical expenses to charitable contributions, there's a whole range of things you can claim as deductions.

But here's the deal – you gotta keep track of your expenses, just like you keep track of your money in the streets. See, the taxman ain't just gonna hand you them deductions on a silver platter. Nah, you gotta do the work and show 'em what you're entitled to.

Let's break it down. Say you been hustlin' hard and had to see the doctor a few times. Them medical expenses, they can add up real quick. But here's the beauty of it – you can claim those medical expenses as deductions, and that means less money gettin' taxed from your hard-earned cash.

And don't forget 'bout them charitable contributions. In the streets, we know how to look out for our community, and the tax game ain't no different. If you been helpin' out them in need and makin' charitable donations, you can claim those as deductions too.

Now, I gotta warn you, my friends. Don't go claimin' deductions you ain't entitled to, 'cause that's a one-way ticket to trouble. The taxman, they watchin', just like them eyes on the streets. Keep it legit, keep it honest, and only claim what you rightfully deserve.

So, here's the deal – keep track of your expenses, gather them receipts, and see if you qualify for them deductions. It's like findin' hidden treasure in the tax game. The more deductions you claim, the less you gotta hand over to the taxman, and that means more dough in your pockets.

And remember, just like in the streets, it's all 'bout bein' savvy and knowin' the game. So, do your due diligence, know your rights, and make them deductions work for you. Keep hustlin', keep stackin', and keep claimin' what's rightfully yours in the tax game!

But be careful, my friend. In the streets, we know that cuttin' corners can lead to trouble. The same applies to taxes. Don't try to claim deductions you ain't entitled to, 'cause the IRS will be on you like a pack of hungry wolves. Keep it legit, and you'll sleep better at night.

In the streets, we know that cuttin' corners ain't nothin' but trouble, and guess what? The same principle applies to taxes.

I get it, we all tryna keep as much of our hard-earned cash as possible, but you gotta do it the right way. Don't be tempted to claim deductions you ain't entitled to, 'cause trust me, the IRS gonna sniff that out like a pack of hungry wolves on the hunt.

The taxman, they ain't playin' around. They got them eyes everywhere, just like them watchful eyes on the streets. They know all the tricks, and if they catch you tryna pull a fast one, you gonna be in for a world of trouble.

So, here's the deal – keep it legit, keep it honest. Claim only them deductions that you rightfully deserve. Don't let greed cloud your judgment, 'cause it's gonna come back to haunt you, and that's a fact.

In the streets, we know how to move smart and stay outta trouble, and the same goes for taxes. Be on the straight and narrow, and you'll sleep better at night, knowin' you ain't gotta worry 'bout them tax wolves knockin' at your door.

Now, I ain't sayin' you can't hustle and claim what's rightfully yours. We all work hard for our money, and we deserve to keep as much of it as we can. But do it the right way, my friend. Dot them I's, cross them T's, and keep your finances clean.

Remember, the tax game, just like the streets, is all 'bout playin' by the rules and stayin' ahead of the game. Don't let greed or desperation lead you down the wrong path. Keep it legit, and you'll come out on top.

So, here's a little hustler's advice – stay true to your grind, keep your money legit, and never forget that cuttin' corners in taxes is a surefire way to land yourself in hot water. Stay smart, stay savvy, and keep hustlin' like the true boss you are!

Now, let's talk about tax credits. In the streets, we know that every dollar counts, and tax credits are like cash in your pocket. They directly reduce the amount of tax you owe, so be on the lookout for any credits you might be eligible for.

In the tax game, every dollar counts, and tax credits are like them secret weapons that directly slash the amount of tax you gotta hand over to the government.

So, listen up, 'cause this is some serious knowledge you wanna have in your arsenal. Tax credits ain't like them deductions that lower your taxable income. Nah, tax credits are like cold, hard cash that gets subtracted straight from your tax bill.

Now, I gotta break it down for you, so you know what's up. See, the taxman, they offer all sorts of tax credits for different things – from takin' care of your family to savin' the environment. There's a whole smorgasbord of credits out there, and it's up to you to be on the lookout for 'em.

Let me give you an example. Say you got kids – them little future hustlers of yours. The government knows that raisin' kids ain't cheap, so they offer a sweet tax credit for that. It's like gettin' a stack of cash back just for doin' what you do best – bein' a parent.

Or how 'bout this – you been investin' in solar panels for your crib, helpin' out the environment and savin' some money on energy bills. Well, guess what? The government rewards you for that too, with a tax credit that puts more money in your pocket.

Now, here's the deal – you gotta know what credits you might be eligible for, 'cause the taxman ain't just gonna hand 'em out like candy on Halloween. You gotta do a little research, see what credits apply to your situation, and claim 'em like the hustler you are.

And let me tell you, my friends, tax credits are the real deal. They ain't just reducin' your taxable income, they're knockin' down your tax bill dollar for dollar. It's like findin' buried treasure out on them streets.

So, don't sleep on them tax credits. Be on the lookout for 'em, claim 'em like a boss, and watch as your tax bill shrinks faster than a snow cone in the summer heat.

Remember, in the streets and in taxes, every dollar counts. So, make sure you're gettin' all them tax credits you're entitled to. It's like puttin' cash back in your pocket, and that's the kind of hustlin' we all wanna do.

In the streets, we know that keepin' good records is essential. In taxes, it's no different. Keep track of your income, expenses, and any documents related to deductions and credits. You don't wanna be caught slippin' when the taxman comes knockin'.

You know how we roll in the streets – keepin' good records is the key to stayin' ahead of the game. And guess what? The same applies to taxes, my fellow hustlers. In this tax game, you gotta be organized like a boss, keepin' track of every dollar comin' in and goin' out.

So, listen up, 'cause this is some real talk you wanna heed. When it comes to taxes, you can't afford to be slippin' or slacking. The taxman, he's like them watchful eyes on the streets, and he ain't gonna take no excuses if you ain't got your paperwork in order.

First things first, you gotta keep tabs on your income. Every hustle, every deal, every dollar – you gotta account for it all. Whether you're out there grindin' in the streets or hustlin' legit in a business, you gotta know where that money's comin' from.

But that ain't all, my friends. You gotta be just as sharp when it comes to your expenses. In the streets, we know how to watch our backs and make sure our money ain't goin' to waste. Well, it's the same with taxes – every expense can be like a valuable asset if you know how to use it.

See, them expenses, they can add up, and they can also be the key to claimin' them deductions we talked about earlier. But if you ain't got the receipts and the records to back 'em up, you might as well be tossin' money into the wind.

And let me tell you, claimin' deductions without proper documentation is like wearin' a target on your back. The taxman, he ain't gonna take your word for it. You gotta have them receipts, them invoices, them documents to prove your case.

Now, I know what you're thinkin' – keepin' all them records sounds like a hassle. But trust me, my friends, it's a small price to pay for stayin' outta trouble. Be organized, be diligent, and you'll be ready when the taxman comes knockin'.

So, here's a little hustler's advice – keep a file, a binder, a digital record – whatever works for you, just make sure you're keepin' them records straight. It's like buildin' a fortress of protection around your money, and that's somethin' every smart hustler knows how to do.

Remember, in the streets and in taxes, you gotta stay sharp and stay on top of your game. Keep track of your income, keep tabs on your expenses, and gather them documents like they're pieces of gold. That way, when the taxman comes knockin', you'll be ready to face him like the true boss you are.

Now, let's talk about hustlin' legally. In the streets, we know that playin' by the rules keeps us outta trouble. The same goes for taxes. Don't engage in shady deals or try to hide your income. The IRS got eyes everywhere, and you don't wanna mess with them.

Listen up, my fellow hustlers, 'cause this is some wisdom you wanna pay close attention to. In the streets, we know that playin' by the rules is the key to stayin' outta trouble, and guess what? The same principle applies to taxes.

Now, I get it – we all tryna get that bag, but you gotta do it the right way. Don't be tempted to engage in shady deals or try to hide your income from the taxman. It might seem like a quick come-up, but trust me, the IRS got eyes everywhere, and they ain't gonna let you slide.

In the streets, we know how to move smart and avoid them sketchy situations. The same goes for taxes. Don't let greed or desperation lead you down the wrong path. Keep it legit, keep it honest, and you'll be a step ahead of the game.

See, the taxman, he ain't just some random dude on the corner. He's like them watchful eyes on the streets, always lookin' out for any sign of foul play. So, don't think you can outsmart 'em or slip under their radar. It's a losing game, my friends.

Now, I know it can be temptin' to try and keep some of that hard-earned cash off the books, but it's a dangerous game to play. The IRS, they got tools, they got resources, and they got ways to catch those who try to cheat the system.

And let me tell you, my friends, the consequences ain't pretty. Fines, penalties, even jail time – it's like steppin' into a trap you can't escape from. You might think you're makin' some extra dough, but in the end, it's gonna cost you way more than it's worth.

So, here's the deal – be a smart hustler, not a shady one. Report all your income, keep your records straight, and don't try to pull a fast one on the taxman. It's like stayin' outta the crosshairs of them rival crews – you wanna keep a low profile and avoid unnecessary heat.

And remember, in the streets and in taxes, you gotta stay one step ahead of the game. Don't let greed or desperation cloud your judgment. Keep it legit, keep it honest, and you'll be on your way to stackin' paper without attractin' any unwanted attention.

So, here's a little hustler's advice – play it smart, stay legit, and you'll be navigatin' the tax game like a true boss. The IRS might be watchin', but that don't mean they gotta catch you slippin'.

Be proactive in managin' your taxes. In the streets, we know that bein' reactive gets you caught. In taxes, don't wait till the last minute to figure things out. Stay on top of your finances throughout the year, so come tax season, you're ready to file like a pro.

In the streets, we know that bein' reactive is a surefire way to get caught with your guard down. It's like waitin' for them rival crews to make their move before you take any action. Nah, that ain't how we roll. We stay ahead of the game, always thinkin' two steps ahead.

Well, it's the same with taxes. Don't wait till the last minute to figure things out. You gotta stay on top of your finances throughout the year. Keep track of your income, your expenses, and all them records we talked about earlier.

See, when you're proactive, you can spot any potential issues before they become problems. It's like sniffin' out trouble before it gets too close. So, when tax season rolls around, you ain't scramblin' like a rookie – you're ready to file like a seasoned pro.

Now, I know it can be temptin' to put off dealin' with taxes. We all got a million things on our plates, and taxes can seem like a headache we wanna avoid. But trust me, my friends, it's a small price to pay for stayin' outta trouble.

Bein' proactive with your taxes is like makin' strategic moves on the streets. It's about protectin' your assets and stayin' ahead of the game. So, make a habit of checkin' in on your finances regularly. Set aside time each month to review your records and see where you stand.

And here's a little tip from a seasoned hustler – use technology to your advantage. There are plenty of apps and software out there that can help you keep track of your money and stay organized. It's like havin' a trusted partner watchin' your back in the tax game.

Remember, in the streets and in taxes, bein' proactive is the key to success. Don't wait for trouble to come knockin' – stay ahead of the game, stay on top of your finances, and you'll be navigatin' the tax game like a true boss.

So, here's the deal – stay sharp, stay proactive, and don't let taxes catch you slippin'!

And yo, consider gettin' some professional help. In the streets, we know that sometimes, you need backup. The same applies to taxes. If you find the whole tax game confusin', consider hirin' a tax professional to help you navigate the maze of rules and regulations.

I get it – taxes can be a whole different language, and it ain't always easy to decipher. But don't let that hold you back. Just like we know when to call in reinforcements on the streets, you gotta know when to bring in the experts for your taxes.

See, a tax professional, they know the game inside and out. It's like havin' a trusted advisor watchin' your back, makin' sure you ain't makin' no costly mistakes. They can help you navigate them tricky tax laws and find them deductions and credits you might've overlooked.

Now, I know what you're thinkin' – ain't no one tryna spend extra money on taxes. But here's the deal – a good tax professional can actually save you money in the long run. They can help you find ways to minimize your tax bill, so you keep more of your hard-earned cash.

Think of it like investin' in yourself – just like we invest in our hustles to see bigger returns. Hirin' a tax pro is like makin' a strategic move to protect your money and your future.

And here's a little secret – a tax pro can also help you plan for the future. They can give you advice on how to structure your finances, so you're set up for success down the road. It's like havin' a seasoned mentor guide you through the tax game.

So, don't be shy about gettin' some professional help with your taxes. It's like bringin' in a heavyweight to your corner for a big fight. You wanna come out on top, and that means havin' the best team behind you.

Remember, in the streets and in taxes, knowin' when to ask for help is a sign of strength, not weakness. So, consider hirin' a tax professional to help you navigate the tax game like a boss.

Now, let's talk about side hustles. In the streets, we know how to stack paper from multiple sources. The same principle applies to taxes. If you're hustlin' on the side, be aware of how it impacts your taxes. Report all your income, whether it's from your main gig or them side hustles.

Let's talk about them tax professionals – these folks know the tax game inside and out. It's like havin' a trusted advisor watchin' your back, makin' sure you ain't makin' no costly mistakes. You know how we always keep our crew close on the streets? Well, a tax pro is like an invaluable part of your financial crew.

They can navigate them tricky tax laws like nobody's business. You know them hidden alleys and shortcuts we use to avoid trouble? A tax pro knows them too, and they can help you find them deductions and credits you might've overlooked.

Now, I know what you're thinkin' – ain't no one tryna spend extra money on taxes, right? But here's the deal – a good tax professional can actually save you money in the long run. It's like makin' a smart investment – you put a little in now, and you reap the benefits later.

See, they can help you find ways to minimize your tax bill, so you keep more of your hard-earned cash in your pocket. It's like increasin' your profits on the streets – we all know how much that means to a true hustler.

And let me tell you, hirin' a tax pro is like makin' a strategic move to protect your money and your future. You know how we always stay ahead of the game, plannin' our moves to avoid any traps? A tax pro can help you do the same with your finances.

Here's a little secret – a tax pro can also be your financial mentor. They can help you plan for the future, set goals, and structure your finances for success down the road. It's like havin' a wise old veteran showin' you the ropes in the tax game.

So, don't be shy about gettin' some professional help with your taxes. It's like bringin' in a heavyweight to your corner for a big fight. You wanna come out on top, and that means havin' the best team behind you.

Remember, in the streets and in taxes, knowin' when to ask for help is a sign of strength, not weakness. So, consider hirin' a tax professional to help you navigate the tax game like a boss. It's like addin' another ace up your sleeve – you never know when it might come in handy.

In the streets, we know that money talks, but so does paperwork. The same goes for taxes. Keep copies of all your tax-related documents, from W-2s to receipts. It's like buildin' an alibi – you wanna have evidence to back up your claims.

Now, let's talk about stayin' in the loop. In the streets, we know that information is power. The same applies to taxes. Keep yourself informed about any changes in tax laws or new deductions that might benefit you. Knowledge is your shield against makin' costly mistakes.

Now, let's talk about filin' your taxes. In the streets, we know that stayin' organized is crucial. The same goes for taxes. Gather all your documents, double-check your numbers, and make sure you ain't missin' anythin'. The last thing you wanna deal with is a tax audit.

But listen, don't let taxes stress you out. In the streets, we know how to stay calm under pressure. The same principle applies to taxes. Take a deep breath, double-check your work, and file your taxes with confidence. If you did your due diligence, you got nothin' to worry about.

Now, let's talk about refunds. In the streets, we know how to celebrate when we come out on top. The same goes for taxes. If you're lucky enough to get a tax refund, don't blow it all at once. Consider puttin' some of it into savings or investin' it for the future.

Now, let's switch gears and talk about givin' back. In the streets, we know that community matters. The same principle applies to taxes. Your tax dollars go toward fundin' important public services, from schools to infrastructure. So, be proud to contribute your fair share.

Now, let's talk about the future. In the streets, we know that hustlin' is about more than just survivin'. The same applies to taxes. Plan for your financial future, whether it's savin' for retirement or buildin' a legacy for your family.

Consider settin' up a retirement account, like an IRA or a 401(k). In the streets, we know that stackin' paper for the long haul is essential. The same principle applies to taxes – prepare for your future self and enjoy the rewards of your hustlin' days.

Now, let's talk about the power of givin' back. In the streets, we know that community matters. In taxes, your contributions go towards fundin' important public services, from schools to infrastructure. So, be proud to contribute your fair share.

And yo, don't forget about charitable contributions. In the streets, we know that givin' back is a way to uplift our community. The same goes for taxes – if you've made donations to eligible charities, you may be able to claim deductions that'll reduce your taxable income.

Now, let's talk about hustlin' smartly with tax-efficient investments. In the streets, we know that strategic moves lead to big payoffs. The same applies to taxes. Explore investment options that offer tax benefits, like tax-deferred retirement accounts or tax-free municipal bonds.

And listen, don't let taxes discourage you from hustlin' and stackin'. In the streets, we know that obstacles are a part of the game. The same applies to taxes. Keep hustlin', keep buildin' your wealth, and use your financial success to create a positive impact in your community.

In conclusion, my fellow hustlers, taxes are a part of life, like it or not. But with a street-smart approach, you can navigate the tax game with confidence. Know your tax bracket, take advantage of deductions and credits, stay organized, and consider gettin' some professional help if needed.

Remember to report all your income, even from side hustles, and stay informed about changes in tax laws. File your taxes accurately and on time, and don't stress over it. If you get a refund, use it wisely, and consider investin' in your future.

Lastly, give back to your community and use your financial success to uplift others. Keep hustlin', stackin', and makin' them money moves like the savvy entrepreneur you are. The streets have taught us to be resilient, and the same resilience will guide us through the tax game. Let's keep on hustlin' and claim that financial success like the true bosses we are!

Building a Legacy

Generational Wealth and Uplifting the Community

Listen up, my hustlin' crew, 'cause we got some serious talkin' to do about buildin' a legacy that stands the test of time. In the streets, we know that every move we make has consequences, and the same principle applies to our finances. It's not just 'bout hustlin' for today – it's 'bout securin' the bag for generations to come.

Generational wealth, my friends, ain't just some fancy buzzword. It's the foundation we lay today that'll empower our kids, grandkids, and beyond. It's about breakin' the cycle of poverty and makin' sure our future generations ain't gotta struggle like we did.

Now, I know what you're thinkin' – ain't nobody talkin' 'bout leavin' behind a trust fund worth millions. Generational wealth can start small, like plantin' a seed that'll grow into a mighty tree. It's 'bout teachin' our kids 'bout money, savin', and investin' so they can build on our legacy.

Take my man, Big Tony, for example. He was a street-savvy hustler just like us, but he had a vision beyond his own gains. He hustled smart, saved wisely, and invested in real estate. And when he passed, he left behind a few properties for his kids.

Now, them properties weren't worth millions back then, but his kids saw the value. They learned the game from their pops, and they kept hustlin', kept buildin'. Fast forward a few decades, and them properties grew into a real estate empire, generatin' wealth for generations.

See, that's the power of buildin' a legacy. It's like plantin' seeds today that'll grow into mighty trees tomorrow. We ain't just hustlin' for ourselves – we're hustlin' to uplift our families, our communities, and our people.

But buildin' a legacy ain't just 'bout makin' money – it's 'bout givin' back too. Remember them roots we talked 'bout in Chapter 16? Well, we gotta use our success to uplift our community. It's 'bout bein' street-smart philanthropists.

You don't need to be a millionaire to give back. Even small acts of kindness can make a difference. Volunteer at local charities, mentor young hustlers, support local businesses – it all adds up.

Let me tell you 'bout my friend, Lil' Tasha. She started from nothin', just like us. But when she made it big in her hustle, she didn't forget where she came from. She used her success to open up a community center for at-risk youth, givin' 'em a chance to break free from the streets.

You see, that's the beauty of hustlin' for a cause beyond yourself. It's 'bout usin' our skills, our resources, to uplift others. We know the struggles of the streets, so we can make a real difference in our communities.

Now, let's talk 'bout growin' that legacy even further. It ain't just 'bout passin' down money, but also passin' down them valuable lessons we learned on the streets. Teach our kids 'bout financial literacy, savin', and investin'.

And it ain't just 'bout our own kids – let's uplift the entire community. Startin' businesses and creatin' job opportunities for our people is like plantin' seeds of empowerment. It's like teachin' others to fish so they can feed themselves for a lifetime.

We know the struggle of survivin' in the streets, so we got the know-how to help others overcome financial hardships. We can offer mentorship and guidance to those tryna make it in this tough world.

Remember, hustlin' ain't just 'bout gettin' paid – it's 'bout buildin' a legacy that'll echo through time. Generational wealth ain't just a dream – it's a reality we can create. So, keep hustlin', keep stackin', and keep buildin' a legacy that'll inspire and empower those who come after us. Our hustle don't end with us – it's the foundation for the future of our families and our community.

Survivin'

Financial Hardships

Resilience in the Face of Adversity

In the streets, we know that life can be tough and unforgivin'. We've seen our share of struggles and hardships, and the same applies to our finances. There are times when the money ain't flowin' like we want it to, and we find ourselves facin' financial challenges head-on.

But let me tell you, my hustlin' crew, it's in these moments that our true grit shines through. It's about survivin' financial hardships with resilience and comin' out stronger on the other side.

We've all been there – times when the hustle ain't bringin' in enough to cover the bills, or unexpected expenses knock us off our game. But we ain't the type to back down. We know how to adapt, how to pivot, and how to keep pushin' forward.

In the streets, we got each other's backs. We form tight-knit crews to watch out for one another, and the same principle applies when times get tough financially. Lean on your support system – your family, your friends, your community. Together, we're stronger than any hardship that comes our way.

Now, let's talk 'bout makin' smart moves during these rough times. Just like we know when to switch up our hustle to stay ahead of the game, we gotta do the same with our finances.

Start by reassessin' your budget – cut out any non-essential expenses and focus on what's truly important. It's like eliminatin' any dead weight that's holdin' you back on the streets. Tighten up your financial game, so you can weather the storm.

And let's not forget 'bout them emergency funds we talked 'bout a couple chapters ago. It's like havin' a stash of cash reserved for rainy days. When unexpected hardships hit, that emergency fund can be a lifesaver.

But sometimes, despite all our hustle and preparation, life can still hit us with curveballs. It's in these moments that we gotta dig deep and summon that hustler's spirit.

Remember, my friends, resilience is the name of the game. It's about pickin' yourself up when you fall, dustin' off your shoulders, and keepin' on movin' forward. We might stumble, but we ain't gonna stay down.

And here's a little hustler's secret – sometimes, askin' for help ain't a sign of weakness. It's like callin' in reinforcements when you're up against a tough crew on the streets. Reach out to local community organizations, charities, or government assistance programs. They might have resources to lend a hand when times get rough.

In the streets, we've faced our share of tough situations. We know how to strategize and outwit our opponents, and the same tactics can be applied to our financial challenges. Look for creative solutions, like hustlin' up a side gig or negotiatin' with your creditors to buy yourself some time.

But beyond the practical moves, it's important to take care of your mental and emotional well-being. Financial hardships can take a toll on your mind, just like the streets can wear you down. Practice self-care, lean on your support system, and find healthy outlets for stress and anxiety.

Remember, every challenge we face is an opportunity for growth. In the streets, we know that every defeat can be a lesson that makes us stronger. Apply the same mindset to your financial struggles – see them as a chance to learn, to adapt, and to improve your financial game.

In the end, it's not just about survivin' the hardships – it's about thrivin' despite them. You got that hustler's spirit runnin' through your veins – use it to propel yourself forward. Embrace the challenge, stay relentless, and keep hustlin' like a true boss.

And when you come out on the other side, share your story with others. Just like we learn from each other's experiences on the streets, our financial journeys can inspire and empower those around us. Be a beacon of resilience and show others that they too can overcome any financial obstacle.

So, my fellow hustlers, embrace the challenges that come your way. Know that financial hardships are just another part of the game we play. We've faced tougher odds on the streets, and we've come out stronger every time.

Remember, it's all about resilience – pick yourself up, stay resourceful, and keep hustlin'. We're in this together, my crew. Let's face these hardships head-on and keep stackin' that paper. Our hustle don't stop, and we don't back down. Keep hustlin', keep stackin', and keep pushin' through the hard times. Our resilience will be our greatest weapon, and it'll lead us to greater heights in the financial game.

Money Talks

Negotiatin' Pay Raises & Better Contracts

right, my hustlin' crew, it's time to talk 'bout a skill that's essential both on the streets and in the financial game – negotiatin'. We know how to work our way around a deal, how to close that sale, and the same tactics apply when it comes to our income.

In the streets, we're always hustlin' for more, and the same principle applies to our paychecks. Don't settle for less when you know you're worth more. Whether you're workin' a 9-to-5 or runnin' your own business, it's time to step up and negotiate that pay raise you deserve.

Now, I know negotiatin' can be intimidatin', but remember, we're hustlers – we fear nothin'. It's all 'bout preparin', presentin' your case, and showin' 'em why you're worth every dime.

Start by doin' your research – just like we scope out our competitors on the streets, find out what others in your field are earnin'. This info gives you leverage when you sit down at that negotiation table.

You can go beyond just salary comparisons. Look into the financial health of your company, industry trends, and the value you bring to the organization. Use data and facts to back up your requests.

Remember, confidence is key – just like we strut our stuff on the streets, walk into that negotiation with your head held high. Speak clearly and assertively, and make your case with conviction.

And don't forget to highlight your strengths – just like we show off our skills on the streets, show your employer or client what you bring to the table. Talk 'bout your accomplishments, your skills, and the value you've brought to the company or project.

But be flexible too – negotiatin' is a give-and-take game. Sometimes, it's not all 'bout the money. You can ask for other perks like flexible hours, remote work options, or additional vacation days. It's like makin' a trade on the streets – you get somethin' you want, and they get somethin' they want.

If your employer is unable to meet your salary expectations, consider other forms of compensation like bonuses, stock options, or additional benefits. Get creative with your negotiations.

And let's not forget 'bout them contracts – whether you're signin' a new deal or renewin' an existin' one, read it carefully. Just like we scrutinize the fine print on the streets, understand every clause and term in your contract.

If there's somethin' you ain't comfortable with, negotiate it. Be firm but fair, and remember, it's all 'bout reachin' a win-win situation.

And here's a little secret – don't be afraid to walk away if the terms don't work for you. Just like we know when to cut our losses on the streets, know when it's time to move on if the deal ain't right.

Sometimes, we gotta be ready to leave a job or a client behind if it's not helpin' us reach our financial goals. Trust your gut and know that there are plenty of other opportunities out there.

Now, let's talk 'bout hustlin' in your own business. Whether you're sellin' products or offerin' services, negotiatin' can make a big difference in your profits.

Price your products or services wisely – don't undervalue yourself, but also be mindful of what the market can bear. It's like findin' that sweet spot on the streets where your customers are happy to pay for what you offer.

And don't forget 'bout them loyal customers – just like we reward our repeat customers on the streets, offer incentives and discounts to keep 'em comin' back for more.

When it comes to business contracts, you gotta protect yourself and your interests. Get everything in writin' – the scope of work, payment terms, deadlines, and any other important details.

It's like makin' sure all parties involved are on the same page, just like we do on the streets when makin' deals.

But beyond just gettin' what you want, buildin' strong relationships is crucial in negotiatin'. It's like formin' alliances with other crews on the streets – it can open up new opportunities and lead to long-term success.

When you negotiate with someone, remember that it's not a one-time transaction. It's the start of a relationship that can benefit both parties in the long run. Be fair, respectful, and trustworthy, and you'll build a reputation as a reliable hustler.

Finally, let's talk 'bout negotiatin' for your dream. If you got a passion project or a big dream you're chasin', don't be afraid to pitch it to potential investors or partners.

Just like we sell our visions on the streets, paint a clear picture of what you want to achieve and how it's gonna benefit them too. Be confident and persistent, 'cause hustlers never back down from a challenge.

Pitchin' your dream is like showin' 'em your hustle – it's your chance to shine and prove that you got what it takes.

Remember, my hustlin' crew, negotiatin' is an art form, and we're masters of it. Whether it's for a pay raise, a contract, or a dream, step up to that negotiation table with confidence and show 'em why you're a force to be reckoned with.

Negotiatin' ain't just 'bout gettin' more money – it's 'bout assertin' your worth, buildin' strong relationships, and makin' strategic moves to advance in the financial game. So, get out there and hustle for every dime you deserve. Keep hustlin', keep stackin', and keep negotiatin' like a true boss.

Hustler's Mindset

Overcomin' Limitations

In the streets and in the financial game, the right mindset can be the difference between success and failure. We know that limitations are like obstacles in our path, but hustlers, we don't let 'em hold us back. It's time to dive deep into the hustler's mindset and learn how to overcome any limitations that come our way.

First and foremost, we gotta believe in ourselves. In the streets, we face doubt and skepticism, but we rise above it all with unwavering confidence. The same goes for our finances. You gotta trust your abilities, trust your skills, and believe that you can achieve whatever you set your mind to.

But let's be real – we all got our share of self-doubt from time to time. When those moments hit, remember the challenges you've already conquered on the streets. Remind yourself of the times you've faced tough odds and came out on top. Use that as fuel to power through any financial challenge.

The hustler's mindset is all 'bout adaptability. We know that the streets can be unpredictable, and we gotta be ready to switch up our game at any moment. The same principle applies to our finances.

Don't be afraid to pivot and try new strategies when it comes to makin' money. Just like we know how to change our approach on the streets, be open to new opportunities and don't get stuck in old ways.

In the financial game, you gotta be willing to take risks too. That might mean investin' in a new venture, startin' your own business, or even negotiatin' for a higher salary.

But here's the key – don't let fear paralyze you. Just like we keep our cool in dangerous situations on the streets, trust your instincts and make informed decisions.

And remember, hustlers don't give up easily. We know that persistence pays off. In the streets, we don't back down from a challenge, and the same goes for our financial goals.

When the going gets tough, stay committed and keep pushin' forward. It's like a marathon on the streets – you gotta pace yourself and keep goin', even when the finish line seems far away.

And don't be afraid to ask for help. Just like we know when to call in our crew for backup, seek advice and guidance from mentors or experts in the financial game.

Remember, no hustler is an island – we all need support and guidance along the way. Reach out to those who've walked the path before you, and learn from their experiences.

But let's also talk 'bout self-discipline. In the streets, we know that stayin' focused and disciplined is crucial to our survival. The same applies to our finances.

Set clear goals and stay disciplined in managin' your money. Create a budget and stick to it, just like we know how to manage our resources on the streets.

And let's not forget 'bout self-education. In the streets, we learn from every experience and keep improvin' our skills. The same mentality applies to our financial knowledge.

Read books, take courses, and stay informed 'bout money matters. The more you know, the better equipped you'll be to make sound financial decisions.

But above all, remember to be kind to yourself. In the streets, we know that we're not perfect, and we make mistakes. It's the same with our finances.

If you stumble, don't beat yourself up. Learn from the experience, dust yourself off, and keep hustlin'. We've all faced setbacks on the streets, but it's how we bounce back that defines us.

And here's the thing, hustlers – it's not just 'bout our own mindset. We can inspire and uplift others to overcome their limitations too.

Just like we motivate our crew on the streets, be a source of encouragement for your friends, family, or colleagues. Share your financial journey, the lessons you've learned, and the successes you've achieved.

Be a role model for others, show 'em that with the right mindset, any limitation can be overcome. Use your own experiences to empower others to take charge of their financial futures.

Now, let's talk 'bout visualizin' success. In the streets, we know that seein' ourselves achieve our goals is a powerful motivator. The same principle applies to our financial aspirations.

Take some time each day to visualize your financial success. See yourself reachin' your financial goals, livin' the life you desire, and stackin' that paper like a true boss.

Visualizin' success is like plantin' a seed in your mind – it grows into a powerful drive that propels you forward. When you can see it, you can believe it, and when you believe it, you can achieve it.

But let's also be real 'bout setbacks – they happen to all of us. In the streets, we know that sometimes, things don't go as planned. The same goes for our finances.

When you face a setback, don't let it discourage you. In the streets, we know that gettin' knocked down ain't the end – it's the gettin' back up that matters.

Analyze what went wrong, learn from the experience, and keep hustlin'. Every setback is an opportunity for growth, for learnin', and for becomin' a better hustler.

And let's not forget 'bout gratitude. In the streets, we appreciate the little things that make life worth livin'. The same applies to our finances.

Practice gratitude for what you have – your health, your skills, your opportunities. Gratitude is like a magnet – it attracts more blessings into your life.

When you're grateful, you're in a positive mindset, and that positivity can lead to financial abundance. Be thankful for every dollar you earn, for every opportunity that comes your way, and for every lesson learned.

In conclusion, the hustler's mindset is a powerful tool in the financial game. Believe in yourself, be adaptable, take calculated risks, and stay persistent. Seek guidance, stay disciplined, and keep learnin'.

Remember, hustlers, we're not bound by limitations – we overcome them. Embrace the hustler's mindset, and let it lead you to financial success. Keep hustlin', keep stackin', and keep pushin' forward like a true boss.

Street-Smart Philanthropy

Givin' Back

Alright, my hustlin' crew, we've talked 'bout stackin' that paper and securin' our financial future, but there's somethin' more to life than just money. It's time to talk 'bout givin' back to our communities and those in need.

In the streets, we know the importance of lookin' out for one another. We form bonds with our crew, and we stand up for our community. The same principle applies to philanthropy – it's 'bout helpin' others and liftin' 'em up.

Now, some may think that philanthropy is only for the wealthy or the privileged, but that ain't true. Hustlers like us know that every little bit counts. It's 'bout givin' what you can, whether it's money, time, or resources.

Start small – just like we take baby steps on the streets, make a difference in your own neighborhood. Volunteer at a local shelter or food bank, or donate to a cause that's close to your heart.

Remember, philanthropy ain't just 'bout money – it's 'bout makin' a positive impact with whatever you got. In the streets, we know that sometimes, a kind word or a helpin' hand can mean the world to someone.

And here's the beauty of it – philanthropy ain't just 'bout helpin' others, it's also good for your own soul. When you give back, you'll feel a sense of fulfillment and purpose that money can't buy.

But let's be smart 'bout philanthropy too. In the streets, we know how to assess risks and rewards, and the same goes for our charitable endeavors.

Do your research – just like we gather intel on the streets, look into the organizations you're supportin'. Make sure they're legit, transparent, and usin' the funds effectively.

And don't forget 'bout impact – in the streets, we know that we ain't got time for empty promises. The same goes for philanthropy – look for causes that are makin' a real difference in the lives of others.

Now, let's talk 'bout usin' our influence for good. In the streets, we got street cred – people respect us 'cause we earned it. The same principle applies to philanthropy – use your influence to inspire others to give back.

Talk 'bout your charitable efforts, share 'em on social media, or even get your crew involved in volunteerin'. Be a role model for others and show 'em that hustlers got heart.

And here's a little secret – philanthropy can also benefit your brand. In the streets, we know how important reputation is, and the same goes for our businesses or personal brand.

When people see that you're givin' back and makin' a difference, they'll respect you even more. Philanthropy can build trust with your customers, clients, or partners, and it can set you apart from your competitors.

But let's not forget 'bout humility – in the streets, we know that ego can be our downfall. The same applies to philanthropy – it's 'bout helpin' others, not boostin' your own ego.

Don't seek recognition or praise for your charitable efforts. Give from the heart, and know that your impact is what matters most.

Now, let's talk 'bout leverage – in the streets, we know how to use our resources strategically. The same principle applies to philanthropy – find ways to maximize your impact.

Consider collaboratin' with other businesses or organizations to tackle big issues together. Pool your resources and skills to make an even bigger difference.

And let's not forget 'bout sustainability – in the streets, we know that long-term success requires careful plannin'. The same goes for philanthropy – look for ways to create lasting change.

Support causes that focus on sustainable solutions, like education, job trainin', or community development. It's like investin' in the future of our communities.

But let's also talk 'bout the power of collective action. In the streets, we know that strength comes from unity. The same principle applies to philanthropy – workin' together can achieve more than any one individual.

Consider joinin' or startin' a philanthropic group or network in your community. By teamin' up with others who share your values, you can pool your resources and amplify your impact.

Now, let's talk 'bout creative ways to give back. In the streets, we know how to think outside the box, and the same goes for philanthropy.

Organize fundraisers, charity events, or awareness campaigns to support your cause. Use your skills and creativity to make a difference in a way that's unique to you.

And don't forget 'bout the power of mentorship. In the streets, we know how important guidance and support can be. The same principle applies to philanthropy – mentorin' others can be a powerful way to make a lasting impact.

Share your knowledge and experience with those who could benefit from it. Offer mentorship or support to individuals or groups who are workin' towards a better future.

In conclusion, philanthropy is a natural extension of the hustler's mindset. It's 'bout helpin' others and makin' a positive impact with whatever you got. Start small, be smart 'bout your giving, and use your influence for good.

Remember, philanthropy ain't just 'bout money – it's 'bout makin' a difference in the lives of others and liftin' up our communities. Keep hustlin', keep stackin', and keep givin' back like a true boss. Together, we can create a better world, one act of kindness at a time.

Passive Income &

Gettin' Paid While Sleepin'

Alright, hustlers, listen up. We've talked 'bout hustlin' hard to stack that paper, but there's another game we gotta play – the game of passive income. See, in the streets, we know how to make money in our sleep, and it's time to apply that same hustle to our finances.

Passive income, my friends, is like the golden ticket in the financial game. It's the money that keeps rollin' in even when you ain't puttin' in active work. It's like havin' a money-making machine workin' for you while you're busy hustlin' on other fronts.

Now, let me break it down for you – there are different streams of passive income, and it's 'bout findin' the ones that work best for you. One of the most common sources of passive income is investments.

Just like we know how to make smart moves on the streets, investin' wisely can generate steady streams of passive income. Whether it's stocks, real estate, or bonds, investments have the potential to grow and pay dividends over time.

But here's the key – passive income ain't a get-rich-quick scheme. It's 'bout long-term thinkin', just like we plan for the future on the streets. You gotta be patient and let your investments grow over time.

And don't be afraid to diversify – just like we know how to spread out our hustles to minimize risk, diversifyin' your investments can protect you from market fluctuations.

Real Estate
The Power of Rental Properties

Now, let's talk 'bout another source of passive income – rental properties. In the streets, we know that real estate can be a solid investment, and it's the same with rental properties.

When you own rental properties, you're collectin' rent every month, even when you ain't there. It's like havin' a crew of money-collectin' soldiers workin' for you while you're on other missions.

But here's the deal – be a responsible landlord. In the streets, we know that treatin' people with respect goes a long way. Take care of your properties and your tenants, and you'll have a steady income stream for years to come.

Start small if you're new to real estate investment – maybe a small residential property or a multi-family unit. As you gain experience and confidence, you can expand your portfolio and grow your passive income.

And here's a little secret – you don't even have to be the one doin' all the work. Consider hirin' a property management company to handle the day-to-day operations. It's like havin' a trusted lieutenant takin' care of your business.

Digital Products & Online Courses

Share Your Knowledge

Now, let's talk 'bout creatin' digital products or online courses. In the streets, we know that sharin' knowledge is a valuable asset. The same principle applies to the online world.

If you got skills, knowledge, or expertise in a particular area, turn it into a digital product or an online course. Once you create it, it can keep generatin' income as people purchase it over time.

And here's the beauty of it – you can create it once and sell it multiple times. It's like havin' a digital hustlin' operation that works while you're busy with other things.

Think 'bout what you're good at – whether it's teachin' a language, sharin' fitness tips, or teachin' people how to start their own businesses. Put together a comprehensive course or package your knowledge into an e-book.

It may take some upfront work to create these digital assets, but once they're out there, they can keep generatin' passive income for years to come.

Affiliate Marketing

Makin' Money with Strategic Partnerships

Now, let's talk 'bout affiliate marketing. In the streets, we know that partnerships can be powerful. The same goes for affiliate marketing.

When you become an affiliate for a product or service, you earn a commission for every sale you refer. It's like havin' a network of money-makers out there workin' on your behalf.

The key to successful affiliate marketing is to promote products or services that align with your brand and your audience. Be genuine in your recommendations, and only promote products you truly believe in.

Look for affiliate programs that offer fair commissions and provide valuable resources for their affiliates. Hustle smart – promote products or services that your audience needs or wants.

And here's a little tip – consider reachin' out to companies you already use or love. Many businesses have affiliate programs, and if you're already a fan, it'll be easier to promote their products.

License Your Work

Turn Creativity into Ongoing Royalties

Now, let's talk 'bout licensin' your work. In the streets, we know that our skills and creativity are valuable. The same goes for creative work.

If you're an artist, writer, photographer, or musician, consider licensin' your work. You can earn royalties whenever your work gets used or reproduced.

It's like gettin' paid for your creativity over and over again. And in today's digital world, there are plenty of opportunities for licensin' your work – from stock photo sites to music libraries.

But here's the key – protect your work. Copyright your creations and use watermarks if needed. In the streets, we know how to protect our territory, and the same applies to your intellectual property.

Automation & Technology

Workin' Smart, Not Just Hard

And don't forget 'bout the power of automatin' your income. In the streets, we know how to work smart, not just hard. The same principle applies to passive income.

Use technology and automation to streamline your passive income streams. Whether it's auto-investing platforms, rental property management apps, or email automation for your digital products – leverage technology to make your money work for you.

But here's the deal – don't get lazy. In the streets, we know that complacency can get us caught slippin'. The same applies to passive income.

Keep an eye on your investments and income streams. Reassess and adjust your strategies as needed. Passive income requires maintenance and occasional fine-tuning.

In conclusion, passive income is like the hustler's dream come true. It's 'bout makin' money while you sleep, while you're hustlin' on other fronts, or while you're enjoyin' life.

> **Invest wisely, diversify, create digital products, leverage affiliate marketing, license your work, and embrace automation and technology to maximize your passive income potential.**

Remember, passive income ain't an overnight success – it's 'bout long-term thinkin' and strategic moves. Keep hustlin', keep stackin', and keep buildin' those passive income streams like a true boss. With the right mindset and hustle, you can achieve financial freedom and a life of abundance. Now, go out there and get paid while you sleep – that's the hustler's way!

Stackin' Wisely

Expanding the Boundaries of Your Wealth

In the never-ending hustle for financial success, we've learned the value of hard work and smart savings. But true mastery of the game lies in diversifyin' yo' portfolio. Like navigatin' through unfamiliar territories, this strategy requires vision and foresight to secure a prosperous future.

The streets have taught us not to rely on a single avenue for our earnings. Similar principles apply to our finances – a diversified portfolio spreads the risks and opens doors to new opportunities.

Investments: Navigatin' the Market's Waves

Just as streetwise maneuverin' helps us avoid trouble, a diversified investment portfolio steers us through the waves of the market. Broadenin' yo' stock holdings across different sectors – technology, healthcare, finance, and more – can cushion the impact of fluctuatin' markets.

Like capturin' prime territories, real estate investments build tangible wealth. Diversifyin' across residential, commercial, and real estate investment trusts (REITs) offers steady income streams and potential appreciation over time.

And let's not forget about strategic development. As we expand our empires, the savvy investor invests in properties with value-add potential, creatin' opportunities for greater returns.

Business Ventures: Cultivatin' a Portfolio of Dreams

In the streets, we know that havin' multiple hustles leads to prosperity. Diversifyin' yo' portfolio with various business ventures follows the same path.

Invest in enterprises spannin' diverse industries, each with its own risk and reward profile. Just like in the streets, strategic alliances with other businesses can forge new territories and open doors to untapped markets.

Virtual Assets: Navigatin' the Digital Frontiers

In the digital age, a diversified portfolio also includes virtual assets. Like explorin' uncharted territories, investin' in cryptocurrency, domain names, or digital art adds an extra layer of potential growth to yo' wealth.

While the virtual world can be unpredictable, doin' yo' research and stayin' informed can help you navigate this ever-evolvin' landscape.

Safety Nets: Weatherin' Life's Storms

In the streets, we know that unexpected challenges arise. Financially, it's essential to build safety nets to weather any storm life throws our way.

Stash away a well-funded emergency fund, akin to a stash of survival gear. It'll keep you grounded during rough patches, ensurin' you can navigate through difficult times with ease.nsurance

Protectin' Yo' Wealth Fortresses

On the streets, we understand the need to protect what's ours. Similarly, health insurance and other forms of coverage safeguard yo' financial fortresses.Like fortifyin' yo' defenses, ensurin' you have proper insurance can shield you from financial catastrophes, keepin' your wealth intact.

International Investments: Expandin' Global Horizons

Just as we're not bound by one neighborhood, a diversified portfolio embraces international investments. Like explorin' foreign territories, investin' in global markets provides exposure to diverse economies and industries.

But tread carefully, as navigatin' international markets requires a keen understanding of currency risks and economic conditions.

Alternative Investments: Uncoverin' Hidden Treasures

Beyond traditional investments, alternative assets offer unique opportunities to diversify yo' portfolio. Consider peer-to-peer lendin', where you become the banker and reap interest payments from borrowers. Or explore the realm of farmland investments, a fruitful frontier with growth potential.

Education & Personal Growth: Investin' in Yo'self

In the streets, we know that continuous improvement is a must. Financially, investin' in yo'self through education and personal growth propels you toward success.

Courses, workshops, and mentorship programs offer opportunities to enhance yo' skills and expand yo' horizons, like explorin' uncharted territories of knowledge.

In conclusion, the art of diversifyin' yo' portfolio is a testament to our strategic abilities. Just as we navigate the streets with savvy foresight, spreadin' our investments across various avenues allows us to weather financial storms and seize new opportunities.

> **Remember, diversification ain't just a strategy – it's an art form, an expression of our financial intelligence. With our street-smart approach, we can build a robust portfolio that stands strong against the winds of change, settin' us on the path to lasting prosperity. Keep hustlin', keep diversifyin', and keep expandin' the boundaries of your wealth!**

Thrivin' with a Wealth Mindset

Thinkin' Long-Term

In the streets, we know that true success ain't just 'bout makin' a quick buck – it's 'bout playin' the long game. Similarly, when it comes to financial success, we must embrace a wealth mindset and thinkin' long-term.

A wealth mindset goes beyond the immediate gains – it's 'bout layin' the foundation for lastin' prosperity. Just like we plan our hustles with strategic precision, we gotta plan our finances for the future.

Investin' in the Future

In the streets, we know that investin' in our hustles pays off big-time. In the same way, a wealth mindset prioritizes long-term investments with growth potential.

Consider investin' in assets that appreciate over time, like real estate or quality stocks. By thinkin' long-term, you give your investments the time to weather market fluctuations and grow exponentiallyEducation

The Currency of Success

On the streets, knowledge is power, and education is the key to new opportunities. Financially, investin' in education equips you with the skills and know-how to navigate the complex world of money.

Take courses on personal finance, investment strategies, and wealth management. The more you know, the more you can make informed decisions that lead to financial triumph.

Plan for Retirement: Securin' Your Legacy

In the streets, we're always lookin' out for the future. Likewise, plannin' for retirement secures your legacy and ensures you can enjoy the fruits of your labor.

Open a retirement account like an Individual Retirement Account (IRA) or a 401(k) plan. By regularly contributin' to these accounts, you build a safety net for your golden years.

Legacy Buildin': Generational Wealth

In the streets, we strive to leave a legacy that lasts beyond our time. Financially, generational wealth is a cornerstone of a wealth mindset.

Consider estate plannin' to pass on your wealth to the next generation. Set up trusts and establish clear inheritances to ensure that your family's future is secure.

Teach the Next Generation: Empowerin' Yo' Tribe

In the streets, we know that knowledge is meant to be shared. Teach the next generation 'bout financial literacy and the principles of a wealth mindset.

Empower yo' tribe to make smart financial decisions from an early age. By doin' so, you break the cycle of poverty and set them on a path to financial success.

Responsible Debt Management

On the streets, we're careful 'bout who we trust. The same principle applies to debt – be discernin' 'bout the debt you take on.

Use debt strategically to build assets or fund opportunities. Avoid reckless borrowin', and ensure that any debt you incur is manageable and serves a clear purpose.

Emergency Funds: Cushionin' Yo' Finances

In the streets, we keep a stash for emergencies. Similarly, a wealth mindset includes buildin' robust emergency funds. Having enough cash set aside can keep you afloat durin' tough times, preventin' you from divin' into debt or sellin' off assets.

Philanthropy: Givin' Back to the Community

In the streets, we take care of our own. A wealth mindset extends this principle to philanthropy – givin' back to the community that supported us.

Find causes that resonate with you and use your financial success to uplift others. Contributin' to charitable endeavors not only makes a difference in the world but also brings personal fulfillment.

Stayin' the Course: Patience and Discipline

On the streets, we know that patience and discipline lead to success. A wealth mindset embraces these virtues as we build our financial empire.

Stay disciplined in your investment approach, avoidin' knee-jerk reactions to market fluctuations. Keep your eye on the long-term goal, knowin' that time is the ultimate ally in growin' wealth.

In conclusion, a wealth mindset is the foundin' stone of lastin' prosperity. Like a true hustler, you must thinkin' long-term and make strategic moves that build a solid financial future.

Invest in education, plan for retirement, and secure generational wealth. Teach your tribe 'bout financial literacy, give back to the community, and stay disciplined in your approach.

Remember, a wealth mindset ain't just 'bout stackin' dollars – it's 'bout buildin' a legacy that'll echo through generations. So, stay committed, stay focused, and stay true to the principles of a hustler's wealth mindset.

The Art of Giving

Philanthropy as a Path to Fulfillment

In the rugged terrain of the streets, we've honed our survival skills and learned the value of unity and compassion. Now, as we stand at the summit of our success, we find ourselves drawn to the art of giving. Philanthropy becomes our canvas, and with each stroke, we create a masterpiece of hope, impact, and fulfillment.

The Power of Purposeful Giving

In the streets, we know that purpose drives our actions. In philanthropy, the power of purposeful giving takes center stage. It's not just about writin' checks – it's about alignin' our resources with causes that resonate with our soul.

Identify the core values that define you as a person. From there, choose charitable endeavors that reflect those values. When you give with purpose, your impact becomes a reflection of your authentic self.

Investing in People and Potential

As career criminals, we've navigated the maze of life, understandin' that people hold the potential for greatness. In the world of philanthropy, we become investors in human potential. Support education programs that nurture young minds, mentorship initiatives that guide the next generation, and community projects that uplift the spirits of those in need. By investin' in people, we create a ripple effect of positive change.

Building Stronger Communities

In the streets, we've seen the strength of unity in buildin' stronger communities. Philanthropy becomes a bridge that connects us with those less fortunate, strengthenin' the fabric of society.

Look to support local nonprofits and organizations that work directly within the communities they serve. Just as we collaborate with allies on the streets, forge partnerships that amplify the impact of your giving.

Engagement and Empowerment

On the streets, we've thrived by actively engagin' with our environment. In philanthropy, the same principle applies – engagement and empowerment go hand in hand.

Participate in volunteer activities to directly connect with the lives you're impactin'. Offer your skills and expertise to make a tangible difference. Just as we take ownership of our hustles, take ownership of the causes you believe in.

Strategic and Sustainable Philanthropy

In the streets, we navigate obstacles with strategic precision. In philanthropy, strategic givin' ensures that our efforts create sustainable change.

Research and vet the organizations you support, ensurin' they have a clear vision and effective strategies. Seek out initiatives that address the root causes of social issues, like we tackle the root of problems on the streets.

Philanthropy with a Global Perspective

As career criminals, we're familiar with diverse territories. In philanthropy, a global perspective expands the horizons of our giving.

Support organizations and projects that address international challenges, like poverty, health, and education. Embrace a worldview that recognizes our interconnectedness, transcending borders to make a global impact.

A Legacy of Compassion and Generosity

In the streets, we're mindful of the legacy we leave behind. In philanthropy, we carve a legacy of compassion and generosity.

Consider establishin' a charitable foundation to carry on your philanthropic mission beyond your time. Just as we build our reputation on the streets, a philanthropic legacy cements your commitment to upliftin' lives.

Philanthropy: A Journey of Self-Discovery

In the streets, we've navigated a path of self-discovery, discoverin' who we truly are. In philanthropy, the journey continues as we explore the depths of our compassion and empathy.

Engage with causes that resonate with your personal experiences and struggles. Just as we draw strength from our challenges on the streets, draw strength from your journey as you give back to the community.

The Joy of Giving Back

In the streets, we know the satisfaction of a successful hustle. In philanthropy, the joy of giving back amplifies that satisfaction to a whole new level.

Experience the joy of seein' lives transformed and communities uplifted through your giving. Like we celebrate victories on the streets, celebrate the impact of your philanthropy with humility and gratitude.

Education and Empowerment: Changin' Lives

As career criminals, we've understood the importance of education and empowerment. In philanthropy, these elements become catalysts for real change. Support initiatives that provide access to quality education, vocational training, and skill development. Just as we empower others to rise on the streets, empower individuals through philanthropy to break the chains of poverty.

The Ripple Effect of Giving

In the streets, we've witnessed the ripple effect of our actions. In philanthropy, every act of giving creates ripples that extend far beyond our immediate impact.

Understand that your philanthropy can inspire others to join the movement. Just as we've been influenced by mentors on the streets, become a guiding light that ignites a passion for giving back in others.

A Philanthropic Ecosystem: Collaboration and Support

In the streets, we've found strength in collaboration and support. In philanthropy, a similar ecosystem emerges, where a network of givers work together for a common cause.

Collaborate with other philanthropists, businesses, and organizations. Just as we've built alliances on the streets, build alliances in the philanthropic world to maximize your collective impact.

In conclusion, philanthropy is the art of giving that enriches our lives and the lives of others. Like true artists, we create a masterpiece of impact and fulfillment through purposeful giving.

> **So, invest in people, build stronger communities, and engage with causes that speak to your heart. Embrace strategic and sustainable philanthropy, and let your giving transcend borders with a global perspective.**

Remember, the art of giving goes beyond material wealth – it's an expression of our compassion, unity, and desire to make the world a better place. Keep paintin' the canvas of philanthropy with colors of hope and love, and let your legacy of compassion shine bright for generations to come.

The Power of Resilient Networks

Forgin' a Supportive Circle

In the hustle of the streets, we've come to know that strength lies not just in individual endeavors but in the power of our networks. As career criminals, we've built alliances and found support in unlikely places. Now, in the realm of philanthropy, we recognize that forgin' a resilient network is essential to createin' a lasting impact and amplifying our efforts.

A Solid Foundation of Support

On the streets, we know that havin' a reliable crew has saved us in tough situations. In philanthropy, surroundin' ourselves with like-minded individuals and organizations forms the foundation of a solid support system.

Build relationships with fellow philanthropists who share your vision and values. Together, we can build a united front, just as we trust our allies on the streets to have our backs. This network becomes the backbone of your philanthropic journey, providing encouragement and support in times of challenges and triumphs alike.

Collaborate for Greater Impact

In the streets, we've seen how collaboratin' can lead to bigger gains. In philanthropy, the same principle applies – workin' together creates a ripple effect of positive change. Join forces with other donors and organizations to tackle complex social issues that may seem insurmountable on your own. Pooling resources and expertise can turn a small effort into a powerful movement, much like we pool resources for a major score. With a collaborative approach, we can address root causes and create systemic change, leavin' a legacy that extends far beyond our own reach.

Mobilizin' Resources Strategically

In the streets, we allocate resources carefully to make the most of our opportunities. In philanthropy, the art of mobilizin' resources becomes a key strategy for effective giving.

Investigate and evaluate various philanthropic initiatives and organizations that align with your values and desired impact. By focusin' on causes that resonate with you personally, you can make strategic choices in givin' to create the change you wish to see. Like we invest in lucrative hustles, invest in initiatives that demonstrate measurable impact and efficiency.

Mentorship and Knowledge-Sharin'

On the streets, we've benefited from the mentorship of those with more experience. In philanthropy, mentorship and knowledge-sharin' play a crucial role in buildin' your philanthropic expertise.

Engage with seasoned philanthropists who can offer guidance and insights, much like we learn from the more experienced hustlers on the streets. By seekin' mentorship and sharin' experiences, you can accelerate your philanthropic journey and avoid common pitfalls. Additionally, consider mentorin' others who are new to the world of giving, passin' on the knowledge and wisdom you've gained along the way.

Amplifyin' Your Message

In the streets, we know the power of spreadin' the word to gain support. In philanthropy, communication becomes a tool to amplify your message and mobilize action.

Utilize social media, public speakin', and other platforms to raise awareness about the causes you support, just like we spread the word about our hustles. By usin' your voice to advocate for positive change, you can inspire others to join the movement and multiply your impact. Share stories of success and the transformative power of your philanthropy to connect with potential donors and beneficiaries on a deeper level.

Diversifyin' Your Impact

In the streets, we understand the risk of puttin' all our eggs in one basket. In philanthropy, diversifyin' your impact ensures a well-rounded approach to givin'.

Consider supportin' a variety of causes and initiatives that align with your values, just as we diversify our hustles to spread the risk. Diversification allows you to address a range of societal challenges, from education to health to environmental sustainability. By castin' a wide net, you increase the likelihood of makin' a significant and lasting difference in the world.

Learnin' from Setbacks

On the streets, we've faced setbacks and learned from our mistakes. In philanthropy, a similar approach is necessary – learn from setbacks and adapt your strategies.

Acknowledge that not every initiative will be an immediate success, and like we evolve our hustles to stay ahead of the game, adapt your philanthropy based on lessons learned from challenges. Conduct thorough evaluations of your projects to identify areas for improvement and make informed decisions about future givin'. By learnin' from setbacks, you can refine your approach and increase the overall effectiveness of your philanthropy.

The Legacy of a Philanthropic Network

In the streets, we aim to leave behind a legacy of respect and influence. In philanthropy, a philanthropic network can be your lasting legacy of impact.

Consider establishin' a foundation or fund that brings together your network under a common mission. Just as we build a reputation that outlasts us, leave behind a philanthropic network that continues to uplift lives for generations. By investin' in the long-term sustainability of your network, you ensure that your philanthropy's impact endures long after you're gone.

In conclusion, forgin' a resilient network in the world of philanthropy becomes the key to multiplyin' our impact. Like we've relied on our connections on the streets, embrace the power of collaboration, mentorship, and resource mobilization to create a movement of positive change.

> **So, surround yourself with a solid foundation of support, collaborate with fellow philanthropists, and strategically mobilize**

> **resources. Mentor and share knowledge, amplify your message, and diversify your impact.**

Remember, in the art of philanthropy, the strength of your network becomes the strength of your legacy. Keep buildin', keep learnin', and keep inspirin' others to join your journey of transformative giving.

In addition to these strategies, consider hostin' fundraisers and events to engage the community and generate support for your philanthropic efforts. Just as we throw parties on the streets to build connections, use events to connect with donors and beneficiaries alike.

Moreover, be open to partnerships with businesses and corporations. Like we find lucrative partnerships on the streets, collaborations with companies can bring additional resources and expertise to your philanthropy.

Beyond monetary support, leverage your network to identify potential volunteers and advocates for your causes. Just as we have lookout brothers on the streets, create a network of committed individuals who are ready to stand by your side in the pursuit of positive change.

Embrace technology and digital platforms to extend the reach of your philanthropy. Like we navigate the digital world for hustlin', utilize online tools and social media to connect with a global audience, spread awareness, and mobilize action for your causes.

In the ever-evolving landscape of philanthropy, continuous learnin' and adaptation are key. Attend conferences, workshops, and seminars to stay informed about best practices and emerging trends. Just as we stay ahead of law enforcement on the streets, stay ahead of the curve in philanthropy to maximize your impact.

Lastly, never underestimate the power of gratitude. Like we show appreciation to our crew on the streets, express gratitude to your donors, partners, and volunteers. A heartfelt thank-you can strengthen your relationships and inspire continued support for your philanthropic endeavors.

In this chapter, we've explored the power of forgin' a resilient network in the world of philanthropy. Like we've mastered the art of connections on the streets, apply these principles to create a network that amplifies your impact, fosters collaboration, and leaves behind a legacy of positive change.

> **So, keep buildin' bridges, keep forgin' alliances, and keep spreadin' the spirit of giving. With a strong**

network behind you, there's no limit to the change you can create.

Knowledge is Power

Educate Yo'self in the Financial Game

In the streets, we know that knowledge is power. It's what separates the successful hustlers from the ones who get caught slippin'. And in the world of personal finance, it's no different. If you wanna stack and prosper, you gotta educate yo'self in the financial game.

Financial Literacy: The Key to Unlockin' Success

Just like we study the streets to know the ins and outs of our hustle, you gotta study the world of finance to make informed decisions. Financial literacy is the key to unlockin' success in the game of money.

Start by learnin' the basics – understandin' how to create a budget, manage debt, and save for the future. Familiarize yo'self with financial terms and concepts, just like we learn the language of the streets. With this foundation, you'll be better equipped to navigate the complexities of personal finance.

But don't stop there. Dive deeper into the world of finance. Learn about different types of investments, from stocks and bonds to real estate and entrepreneurship. Understand the power of compound interest and how it can work for you. Explore the intricacies of tax laws and how they can impact your financial decisions.

Resources for Learnin'

In the streets, we know the importance of havin' the right connections. In the world of financial education, seek out the right resources to expand yo' knowledge.

There are plenty of books, courses, and online resources that can teach you about personal finance. Just as we seek advice from experienced hustlers, look for guidance from financial experts who have been in the game and know the ropes.

Attend financial seminars and workshops to gain insights from professionals and connect with like-minded individuals. Join online forums and discussion groups to exchange ideas and learn from others' experiences. Like we network with other hustlers, network with those who can support and enrich your financial journey.

Stayin' Up-to-Date

In the streets, we know that things can change in a heartbeat. To stay ahead of the game, you gotta stay up-to-date with the latest trends and developments. The same goes for personal finance.

Keep an eye on financial news and updates, like we keep an eye on the streets for any signs of trouble. Be aware of changes in tax laws, investment opportunities, and economic trends that may impact your financial decisions. Like we adapt our hustles to stay relevant, adapt your financial strategies to align with the ever-changing landscape.

Subscribe to financial publications and newsletters to receive regular updates. Follow reputable financial websites and blogs to stay informed about the latest happenings in the world of finance. Attend conferences and webinars hosted by financial experts to gain valuable insights and stay current with industry trends.

Learn from Others' Mistakes

In the streets, we learn from the mistakes of others to avoid makin' the same ones ourselves. In personal finance, take the same approach – learn from others' mistakes to make wiser choices.

Read about financial pitfalls and stories of individuals who faced financial challenges, like we analyze past hustles to avoid similar mishaps. Understand the consequences of mismanagin' money, like we understand the consequences of missteppin' in the streets. By learnin' from others' experiences, you can avoid costly errors and protect your financial future.

Look for case studies and testimonials of people who have achieved financial success through wise money management. Seek inspiration from those who have overcome financial obstacles and turned their lives around. By takin' in these lessons, you can build a more robust financial plan and set yourself up for long-term prosperity.

Resilience

Bouncin' Back from Setbacks

In the streets, we know that no matter how skilled you are, setbacks are a part of the game. It's not about avoidin' them, but how you handle 'em that defines your success. In the world of personal finance, resilience is a crucial trait for navigatin' the ups and downs of the financial journey.

Embracein' the Hustler's Mindset

In the streets, we've faced our fair share of obstacles. It's not always smooth sailin', and we've learned that adaptability and a hustler's mindset are essential for survival. In personal finance, the same principles apply – embrace the hustler's mindset and be ready to pivot when challenges arise.

When faced with financial setbacks, don't be discouraged. Keep a positive attitude and see setbacks as opportunities to grow and learn, like we see setbacks on the streets as chances to evolve our strategies. Hustlers don't give up when the going gets tough; we persevere and find creative ways to overcome obstacles.

Maintainin' a Solid Financial Plan

In the streets, we know that plannin' is a vital part of any successful hustle. In personal finance, a solid financial plan is your roadmap to navigate through difficult times.

Create a budget that accounts for unexpected expenses and emergencies, like we budget for potential risks on the streets. Set aside funds for an emergency savings account, just as we stash away reserves for unforeseen circumstances.

By havin' a well-thought-out financial plan, you'll be better prepared to weather financial storms and avoid makin' rash decisions that can lead to further setbacks.

Learnin' from Setbacks and Mistakes

In the streets, we learn from our mistakes to avoid repeatin' them. In personal finance, it's essential to reflect on setbacks and identify areas for improvement.

If a financial decision didn't turn out as planned, analyze what went wrong and learn from the experience. Be honest with yourself about any missteps, like we analyze our hustles to find room for growth. By doin' so, you can refine your financial strategies and make wiser choices in the future.

Resilient Hustler, Resilient Investor

In the streets, we understand that each hustle comes with risks. We mitigate those risks by diversifyin' our activities and investments. In personal finance, diversification is just as important to buildin' resilience.

Diversify yo' investment portfolio to spread risk across different assets and industries, like we diversify our hustles to avoid puttin' all our eggs in one basket. By doin' so, you reduce the impact of any single setback on yo' overall financial well-bein'.

Bein' prepared for financial downturns requires a long-term perspective. Just as we play the long game on the streets, maintain a focus on yo' long-term financial goals and avoid makin' impulsive decisions based on short-term fluctuations.

Lean on Yo' Support Network

In the streets, we rely on our crew for support and encouragement. In personal finance, lean on yo' support network for guidance and assistance durin' tough times.

Seek advice from financial advisors, mentors, or friends with financial expertise, just as we rely on experienced hustlers for guidance. Discussin' yo' financial challenges and goals with others can provide valuable insights and perspective.

Durin' times of difficulty, don't hesitate to reach out for help, like we rely on our crew in times of need. Whether it's seekin' financial advice or emotional support, surround yo'self with people who have yo' best interests at heart.

Buildin' Resilience for Generational Wealth

In the streets, we aim to leave a legacy for the next generation. In personal finance, buildin' resilience is crucial for creatin' generational wealth.

Teach yo' children and family members about the importance of financial resilience, just as we pass down hustlin' knowledge to the next generation. Educate them about money management and the value of savin' and investin'. By equipin' them with financial skills, you empower them to face future challenges with confidence.

Establishin' a Lastin' Legacy

In the streets, we know that our actions and choices define our legacy. In personal finance, the legacy you leave goes beyond money – it's about the impact you make on others.

Consider how yo' wealth and success can be used to give back to the community, like we use our resources to support our crew. Engage in philanthropy and charitable endeavors to uplift those in need.

By buildin' a legacy of generosity and resilience, you'll be remembered not only for yo' financial success but also for the positive change you brought to the lives of others.

Practicin' Mindfulness and Mental Resilience

In the streets, we rely on mental toughness to navigate through challenging situations. In personal finance, developin' mindfulness and mental resilience is equally important.

Stress and anxiety can accompany financial setbacks, just like we face stress in the streets. Practice mindfulness techniques to stay present and focused, reducin' stress and improvin' decision-makin'.

Understand the difference between reactin' emotionally to financial challenges and respondin' thoughtfully. By cultivatin' mental resilience, you can approach financial setbacks with a clear mind and make rational choices.

Continuin' to Learn and Adapt

In the streets, we never stop learnin' and adaptin'. The same applies to personal finance. Stay abreast of the latest financial trends, technologies, and opportunities, just like we stay updated on the latest developments on the streets. Be open to new ideas and approaches, like we're open to experimentin' with new hustles.

Continuin' to educate yo'self and adapt yo' financial strategies can help you stay ahead of the game and build resilience against unforeseen circumstances.

Remember, in the streets and in personal finance, setbacks are inevitable, but resilience is the key to bouncin' back and thrivin'. Embrace the hustler's mindset, learn from setbacks, diversify yo' investments, and lean on yo' support network.

Teach the next generation about financial resilience and use yo' success to leave a lastin' legacy of generosity and positive change. Practice mindfulness to stay mentally resilient and keep educatin' yo'self to adapt to an ever-evolvin' financial landscape.

In the next chapter, we'll delve into the art of negotiatin' and how it can help you save money and make wise financial decisions. Stay tuned, and let's keep hustlin' and stackin' with resilience and determination.

Bag Secured

Celebratin' Success

In the streets, we know that every win, no matter how small, is worth celebratin'. In personal finance, celebratin' yo' financial successes is just as important. Secure the bag and give yo'self credit for the progress you've made on yo' journey to prosperity.

Appreciatin' the Journey

In the streets, we're always hustlin', strivin' for more. But in the pursuit of financial success, don't forget to appreciate the journey, like we cherish every step of our hustlin'.

Reflect on where you started and how far you've come, just as we look back on our beginnings. Whether you've paid off debt, saved a significant amount, or made a successful investment, acknowledge and celebrate yo' achievements.

It's easy to get caught up in chasin' bigger goals, but takin' time to appreciate yo' progress will keep you motivated and remind you of yo' capabilities.

Rewardin' Yo'self

In the streets, we treat ourselves after a successful hustle. In personal finance, rewardin' yo'self for yo' financial achievements is a way to stay motivated and maintain a healthy relationship with money.

When you reach a financial milestone, like payin' off a loan or reachin' a savings goal, treat yo'self to somethin' you enjoy, just as we reward ourselves with a little splurge after a successful hustle.

However, balance is key. Celebrate responsibly and avoid underminin' yo' progress by overspendin'. A small reward can be a powerful motivator without derailin' yo' financial plans.

Recognizin' Yo' Support Network

In the streets, we know we can't succeed alone. Our crew has our back, and we have theirs. In personal finance, recognize and acknowledge yo' support network.

Yo' family, friends, mentors, and financial advisors may have played a crucial role in yo' financial journey, just as our crew supports and guides us in the streets. Show appreciation for their encouragement and assistance.

Share yo' successes with yo' support network, just as we share our triumphs with the crew. Celebrate together and build a sense of community around yo' financial achievements.

Set New Goals

In the streets, we're always plottin' the next move. In personal finance, settin' new goals after celebratin' yo' successes keeps you focused and motivated.

Set realistic and achievable financial goals, just as we set specific targets for our hustles. Whether it's savin' for a dream vacation, startin' a business, or buildin' a retirement fund, set targets that align with yo' financial vision.

Break down yo' goals into smaller milestones, like we tackle smaller hustles on the way to a bigger score. Celebrate each milestone, and as you progress, adjust and set new goals to keep growin'.

Sharin' the Knowledge

In the streets, we pass down knowledge to the next generation of hustlers. In personal finance, share yo' knowledge and experience with others who may be on a similar journey.

Be open to discussin' financial strategies and offerin' advice, like we share tips and tricks with up-and-comin' hustlers. Encourage financial literacy and empower others to take control of their financial futures.

By sharin' what you've learned, you're contributin' to the financial well-bein' of others, just as we contribute to the success of our crew by sharin' hustlin' wisdom.

Continuin' to Hustle and Stack

In the streets, we never stop hustlin'. In personal finance, continuin' to hustle and stack ensures you keep makin' progress.

Stay disciplined with yo' budget and financial plan, just as we stay disciplined in our hustles. Keep investin' in yo'self and yo' future, like we invest in our skills and knowledge.

Celebrate yo' successes, but don't rest on yo' laurels. Stay driven and committed to achieve even more, like we're always lookin' for the next big score.

Remember, celebratin' yo' financial successes is more than just patting yo'self on the back. It's about appreciatin' the journey, rewardin' yo'self responsibly, and recognizin' the support of others.

Set new goals, share yo' knowledge, and keep hustlin' and stackin' to build a secure financial future. In the next chapter, we'll explore the art of negotiatin' and how it can help you save money and make wise financial decisions. Stay tuned, and let's keep celebratin' the wins on our path to financial prosperity.

Don't Hope.

Hustle.

As we come to the end of this street-smart guide to personal finance, I hope you've gained valuable insights and inspiration from my journey as a career criminal turned financially savvy individual. From hustlin' on the streets to stackin' wealth, the principles that guided me can help you navigate the complexities of personal finance with confidence and determination.

Remember, in both the streets and personal finance, success comes to those who stay focused, adaptable, and resilient. Embrace the hustler's mindset, be resourceful, and never shy away from a challenge. Celebrate every win, no matter how small, and use setbacks as opportunities for growth and learning.

Just like I've emphasized throughout this guide, knowledge is power. Educate yourself about money matters, seek financial literacy, and never stop learnin' and improvin'. Stay disciplined with your finances, build a solid financial plan, and diversify your investments to secure your financial future.

And don't forget to give back. As you prosper, uplift others in your community and be a positive force for change. Philanthropy and generosity are not just acts of kindness; they are investments in a brighter and more equitable future.

Lastly, don't be afraid to seek help and guidance when needed. Just as I've relied on my crew in the streets, surround yourself with a supportive network and consider enlisting the expertise of financial professionals to navigate the complexities of taxes, investments, and money management.

I hope this guide has inspired you to take control of your financial destiny and set yourself on the path to generational wealth. Remember, you have the power to shape your future and create a lasting legacy for yourself and your loved ones.

So, embrace the Hustler's Oath - thrive, inspire, and secure the bag. May you continue to hustle, stack, and prosper, and may your journey be filled with success, resilience, and the fulfillment of your dreams.

With the knowledge gained from the streets and the wisdom of financial prosperity, you have the tools to make a difference. Let's keep hustlin', keep growin', and keep stackin' - together.

Thank you for embarking on this journey with me. Now, go out there and conquer the world, one hustle at a time. Stay true to the hustler within you and remember, the hustle never stops. Keep hustlin', and may success be yours always.

-Max "Stacks" Johnson

'23

About The Author

Connor "*Con-Vict*" Victorious

Emerging into the world during a Crimson Lunar Eclipse and constrained by imprisonment for the majority of his existence, Connor Victorious honed the craft of credit manipulation in the midst of obscurity. Possessing a intellect as keen as the makeshift blades he once bore behind bars, he wove narratives that elicited uneasy laughter even from the most unyielding detainees. Today, liberated from tangible restraints, his prose unveils delightfully unsettling visions and spine-tingling amusement, all the while his credit enchantments aid others in breaking free from financial chasms. Step into his domain, find merriment within the shadows, and contemplate your personal emancipation.

Books By This Author

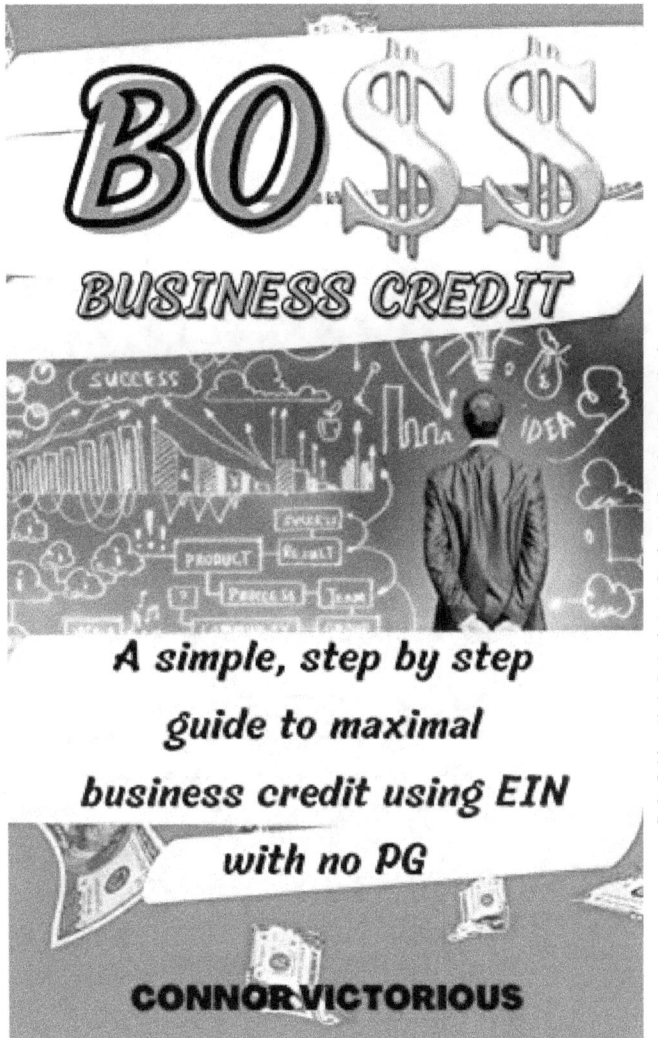

Boss Business Credit

A Simple Step by Step Guide to Maximal Business Credit Using EIN With No PG

A no-B.S. step-by-step approach to building business credit without using your social security number, and without needing a personal guarantee. Follow each step to the "T" and you will have more success in your life than you know what to do with.

-How to name your business

-Best business structure to get credit

-What information gets reported and where it gets reported

-Companies that extend credit automatically

-How to properly set up your business to receive business credit, even if you have horrible personal credit

-How and when to apply for business bank accounts

-How to pay your Vendors using a credit card even if they do not accept credit cards

-Exactly how and what info to include when you create your business

-Tradelines you should apply for and the specific requirements needed to be accepted

....and so much more!

No chapters! No side notes! No filler! No B.S.!

Get the most credit for your businesses in the least amount of time possible! All delivered in a step-by-step, linear instructional that anyone can follow.

AVAILABLE NOW ON AMAZON.COM

BOSS BUSINESS CREDIT

Auto Financing with No Personal Guarantee

Get Car Loans Using Only Your EIN

Get multiple vehicles using business credit ONLY.
An entire fleet of vehicles using only your EIN...No SSN!
No Personal Guarantee!
No Proof of Business Revenue!
Using estimated monthly income!
No documentation!
Use this technique to start your own Auto-Rental Business.
Start making $800 per car OVER the monthly payments of the cars.
Imagine having 10 cars in your fleet; all of them bought using your business credit!

In this book, we will discuss which banks and financial institutes will accept you using your business credit only to qualify for purchasing vehicles.
It IS possible when done right.
You can get auto loans using your EIN only and not your SSN.

AVAILABLE NOW ON AMAZON.COM

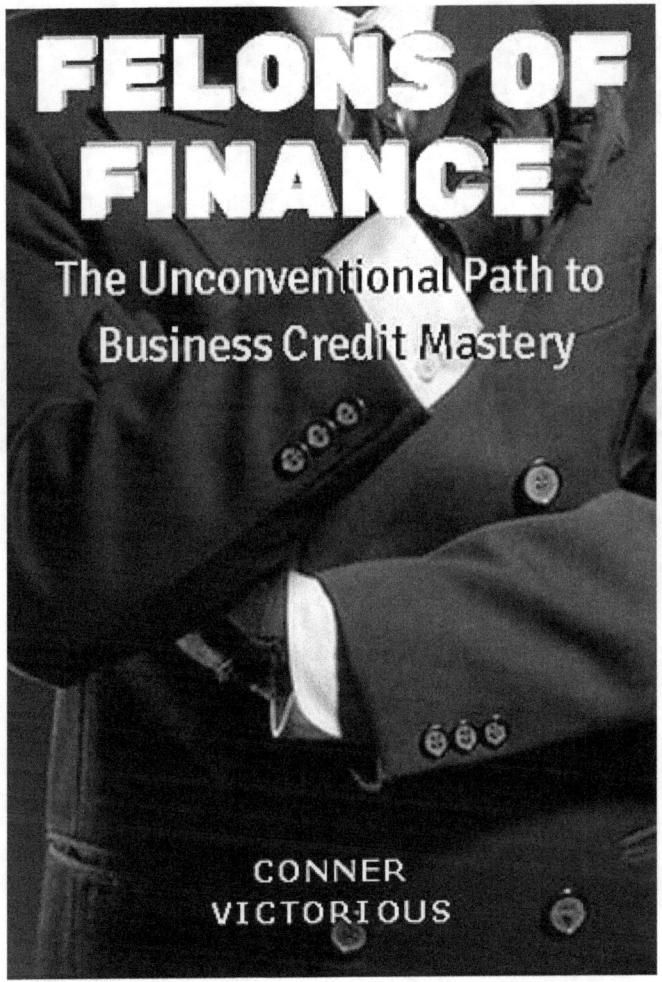

Felons of Finance

An Unconventional Path to Business Credit Mastery

Welcome to "Felons of Finance: An Unconventional Path to Business Credit Mastery." Get ready to dive deep into a world where the impossible becomes possible through *cunning tactics, loopholes, and "legal gray areas"*. We'll show you how to use business credit to open doors you never dreamed of, breaking free from the limitations of your personal credit history.

This ain't your average guide; we're gonna show you how to walk the line between the *"legal"* and the *"unlawful."* Caution and creativity will be your partners as you learn to push the boundaries while staying one step ahead of the law.

Are you ready to *break the chains, embrace creativity, and unlock a world of limitless possibilities*? Join us on this wild ride. "Felons of Finance" will turn you into a *business credit virtuoso*, bending the rules with finesse and redefining the meaning of financial success. Let's get started on this thrilling journey to a *life of abundance and power*!

AVAILABLE NOW ON AMAZON.COM

For more info on this book or about the author visit:

www.felonyfreedomllc.com

There you will find more resources such as:

-easy business loans

- business formation

-consignment

-consultation

- and much more!

We are felon-friendly and will provide assistance in any way possible.

Www.felonyfreedomllc.com

www.ingramcontent.com/pod-product-compliance
Lightning Source LLC
Chambersburg PA
CBHW062323290526
45794CB00005B/1871